A brief history of thrift

Thoreau – 1817–1862
Ghandi – 1869–1948

Manchester University Press

A brief history of thrift

Alison Hulme

Manchester University Press

Copyright © Alison Hulme 2019

The right of Alison Hulme to be identified as the author of this work has been asserted by her in accordance with the Copyright, Designs and Patents Act 1988.

Published by Manchester University Press
Altrincham Street, Manchester M1 7JA
www.manchesteruniversitypress.co.uk

British Library Cataloguing- in- Publication Data
A catalogue record for this book is available from the British Library

ISBN 978 1 5261 2883 6 hardback
ISBN 978 1 5261 5596 2 paperback

First published 2019

The publisher has no responsibility for the persistence or accuracy of URLs for any external or third- party internet websites referred to in this book, and does not guarantee that any content on such websites is, or will remain, accurate or appropriate.

Typeset by Newgen Publishing UK

For Ada

Contents

List of figures	*page* viii
Preface	ix
Acknowledgements	xii
Introduction	1
1 Towards a theory of thrift	6
2 Religious thrift: Puritans, Quakers and Methodists	17
3 Individualist thrift: Benjamin Franklin, Samuel Smiles and Victorian moralism	35
4 Spiritual thrift: simplicity, sensuality and politics in Henry Thoreau	53
5 Nationalist thrift: making do, rationing and nostalgic austerity	69
6 Consumer thrift: Keynes, consumer rights and the new thrifty consumers	79
7 Ecological thrift: frugality, de-growth and Voluntary Simplicity	92
Conclusion: Thoreau in the city	108
Afterword	118
Notes	119
References	127
Index	138

Figures

4.1 Thoreau's cabin as drawn by his sister Sophia for the
    original title page of *Walden* (public domain) *page* 55
5.1 'Dig for victory' poster from the Second World War
    (public domain) 70
5.2 'Make do and mend' poster from the Second World War
    (public domain) 71
6.1 Members of the Brains Trust pictured with Roosevelt
    in 1932 (public domain) 82
7.1 The Global Village Construction Set: the fifty machines needed
    to build a small civilisation (public domain) 97

Preface

When I was a child we used dusters cut from our old clothes, made worn-out trousers into shorts, and collected the tin-foil milk bottle tops for recycling. Bed sheets were 'side to middled' when they wore out; leftovers were always cooked up the next day; even Christmas wrapping paper was carefully saved for the following year. This was not because I came from a particularly mean, moral or even poor family – although money was always a background concern – it was simply because in our house that was how things were done. Whilst some of my friends with younger parents grew up with a far greater engagement with the consumer culture of the 1980s, the influence of wartime thrift on the generation of *my* parents had been strong and irreversible. It did not dissipate simply because the rationing and making do put in place during the Second World War had stopped, and economic conditions improved. Their parents had passed on thrifty habits to them, and their young lives had been affected by the rationing that continued after the war. Thrift was a way of life, a principle, and it came with its own small senses of pleasure. My mum still enjoys being thrifty in small ways; enjoys the feeling that she has made everything useful and wasted nothing, for its own sake, not even to save money really, as the difference would be negligible. For her and many others, being thrifty is about a sense of self-sufficiency more than anything; a comforting sense of not needing too much, of being able to be happy making do. Perhaps what lies behind this for many people is a sense that one is in control as much as is possible of one's situation; a sense that fluctuations in one's economic situation would not necessarily hit one too hard; and a sense of a kind of freedom and therefore happiness that comes with that. Certainly, for my mum, and many like her, thrift has become an embedded part of her identity; the principled, practical habit of a lifetime, despite the changes in attitudes towards consumerism in the postwar era.

Of course, this inevitably had an effect on me. When I was a child, my mum often said (and still does), 'I wouldn't buy that/waste that even if I had a million pounds', and I feel exactly the same. I too take pleasure in making use of every last bit of something, and of re-using things in new ways if at all possible. Throughout my life so far, I have often needed to be extremely thrifty for financial reasons, but this does not go far enough in explaining the real reasons I do it, and certainly does not explain why I get so much pleasure from it. That, I am sure, comes from the same sense of freedom and the associated happiness I mentioned above, and is broadly aligned to the motivations of the many people across the Western world who attempt to simplify, downsize and become self-sufficient. However, it does not explain things enough and, in writing this book, I have been forced to consider my own attitudes and behaviour when it comes to thrift more deeply, and in light of various powerful historical strands. I am painfully aware that on one hand I take a harsh attitude towards the preaching of thrift to the less well-off and indeed towards any moralising discourse of it. I resent those in positions of greater economic or political power telling others (whose lives they usually have little to no understanding of) how to live – especially when that telling is for the success of the nation as part of an apparently collective effort, falsely sold. It seems to me that the effort frequently falls to those least able to realistically make it, whilst nothing is required of those for whom it would be easiest. On the other hand, I myself come from, and perpetuate, a thinking and practice which cannot help but be embedded to some extent in moral discourses. I do tend to think that many people would be happier, and the world would be on a better ecological footing, if we wasted less/needed to buy less and therefore earn less/had more time to enjoy life, and I cannot really deny that this is in some way a moral stance.

So where does that leave me? In many ways, as the introduction of this book will explain, this uneasy position is thrown up by the changes in the way the word thrift is used. The thrift I enjoy is based on the older etymological understanding of the word – that of thriving. The thrift I resent is based on the more recent usage of the word – that of frugality (especially that placed on people for false reasons). Even then, I still find myself wriggling around uncomfortably with my own rationale for enjoying thrift. Thrift as thriving tends to be such a singularly individual pursuit, and one that only those who already have enough can engage in. This thrift, whilst garnering the support of sizeable pockets of people across the Western world, is unlikely to challenge the way society is run. It is a luxury pursuit in many ways, and it makes me slightly uneasy. The emphasis on personal happiness is perfectly valid, but it is not enough. It is precisely related to a sense of *personal* freedom, but has little to do with challenging societal inequality and a wider sense of freedom for the many. Those who adhere to it like to imagine that if they lead by example, others will follow, but even if this were the case it would not lead to wide-scale wealth redistribution. It is essentially a thrift based on individual choice and too easily hijacked by the logic of neoliberal economics.

What this book hopes to expose is how thrift as thriving became quite so wholeheartedly embroiled in thrift as a capitalistic practice of frugality. In doing so, it explores key historical strands of thought, and certain historical characters who have been amongst the finest purveyors of thrift (of both the thriving and the frugal variety), attempting to sift through these with the aspiration of finding a thrift more committed to solidarity rather than individualism, and more able to change everyday life for the many. From analysing this strange and wonderful array of people and ideas, it turns out that it is perhaps not a 'romantic ethic' of hedonistic desire to consume that has fed the 'spirit of capitalism' (as Colin Campbell famously argues), but rather a pragmatic ethic of desire for economic freedom through thrift. Thrift has at once defined itself against capitalism and for capitalism and regardless has in reality ended up working for it on almost all occasions. But this is not to say the idea is unsalvageable – far from it. For example, radical ecologists are making great strides towards a more collectively defined thrift that carves out new structures and ways of being. And history reveals subtleties within the work of more conventional thrift advocates that are useful for an alternative future conception of thrift. There is, then, a slightly utopian aspect to this book (for which I am unapologetic), or at least to the place it ends up, in that it is attempting to draw together a way forward for thrift that has practical implications – that is, if you like, a blueprint for a way of living. The blueprint itself is certainly a whole other project, but for now, I hope this book pulls apart logics that have been wrongly glued together for far too long and challenges in a small way some of the long-held 'truisms' about the nature of capitalism.

Acknowledgements

Thanks as always to close friends and family for love and laughter and the maintenance of sanity.

Introduction

At the conclusion of my last book – *On the Commodity Trail* – I asserted that consumptive thrift (i.e. that which essentially still encourages spending, but as part of seeking a 'bargain') was, in the current age, the only type of thrift fully condoned by those in positions of power in the West. Furthermore, I argued, it was used to obscure the fact that trickle-down economics have failed both the developed and the developing world. Consumptive thrift, I argued, required people to consume; insisted upon itself as an activity engaged in, not in order to save money by not spending, but in order to save money *on purchases* by being a wise consumer. It is, essentially, Keynesian thrift. In addition, this ability to be 'wise' in one's consumptive choices has been extended to goods and services that people had previously not been 'customers' of, but rather, students, patients or tenants, for example. It has been used as a tool in the plotted gradual decline of welfare provision and any attempt at genuinely collective responsibility. In many ways, this book follows on from where that one left off – by looking exclusively at the concept of thrift and the way it has been used politically to encourage and discourage certain socio-economic behaviours throughout history. It seeks to understand how the concept of thrift has been used and abused over time, and how the thrift-seeking/thrift-avoiding individual subject has been celebrated and chastised accordingly. It is then, part archaeology of thrift – mining into the uses of a concept; and part anthropology of thrift – exploring how interpretations of the concept have resulted in specific forms of everyday life. More crucially, it attempts to pick apart the relationship between capitalism and thrift and assert thrift, as its own practice, in its own right, not only as capitalism's handmaiden (although acknowledging this role), but as its historically ever-present Other.

This book is not a historical treatise, robustly covering all periods. Experts on any of the historical periods or characters that feature in it will have little to gain from it in terms of furthering their historical knowledge. It is not chronological in any strict sense. And it leaps across geographic boundaries without worrying too much about a 'scientific' tracing of influence. Instead, it attempts a thematic exploration of the concept and practice of thrift via influential characters and specific eras and movements in which it has proved a particularly potent concept. This is to address Lendol Calder's suggestion that in attempting to chart the history of thrift, historians (which I am not!) would ideally 'find it possible to move beyond familiar rise and fall narratives in which parsimonious saving is invented by the Puritans, achieves its greatest influence among the Victorians, and then in the late twentieth century withers away and dies'. He asks that we propose 'more complex narratives of institutional and cultural realignment in which the meaning and practice of thrift ebbs and flows across time and form place to place, buffeted by historical transformations yet capable of being revived and realigned in manifold, often cross-cutting ways of restraint and release' (2013:363).

As a result, this book considers thrift through movements as diverse as Puritanism, Keynesianism and Voluntary Simplicity, and through characters as unaligned as Benjamin Franklin, Franklin D. Roosevelt and Henry Thoreau. Yet, it finds, in tracing these strands of thought, that sometimes ideas end up in unexpected places and have effects in the present that could never have been predicted. Who would have thought, for example, that the transcendentalists of the nineteenth century would have been the influence behind both Samuel Smiles and Henry Thoreau – two characters that could not appear more different from each other? Who would have predicted that John Wesley's belief in working hard, saving and giving away would inform much of the US Voluntary Simplicity movement? Who could have foreseen that a discourse beset by the individualism and charitable awareness of the Victorian era would rear its head in new forms today as a rationale for the destruction of the welfare state?

Such apparent anomalies are testament to the way in which thematic trends enter and exit history at various unexpected points, and actors consistently borrow (often without even realising they are doing so) from their predecessors. So, this book is historical, but not a work of history in the traditional sense; rather, it is of overlapping lines of historical influence in which thrift(s) become entwined in unusual and unlikely ways. As Yates and Hunter argue, there was no simple ascent and decline of thrift; they emphasise instead the complexities of institutional and cultural realignment that enabled it to survive in various forms throughout history. For them, thrift has proved itself to be a remarkably dynamic and versatile concept and practice, concerned at various historical moments with 'human survival, religious calling, political independence and self-rule, environmental conservation, racial hegemony, philanthropy, manhood and womanhood, collective security, and social protest' (2011:10). Regardless, Calder's contention remains true – 'no concept has been more important than thrift for shaping the moral culture of economic life under capitalism' (2013:363).

It is also worth noting that this book is largely about Western thinkers on, and versions of, thrift. There is a tangible historical conversation between the Western and the non-Western world, and Western and non-Western thinking do get blurred now and again along the way (Thoreau's influence on Gandhi being a classic example), so now and again, non-Western thinkers have small walk-on parts. However, the specific shifts from thrift as thriving to thrift as frugality, and vice versa, are intricately linked with Western thought, largely due to the way in which thrift has played such a specific part in the development of Western capitalism. Thrift, on the whole, cannot be understood in the same way when viewed from a non-Western context. Therefore, this book only attempts to deal with thrift in the Western context, although future writings may well attempt to delve into those non-Western thinkers for whom thrift played an important role as there is undoubtedly a very interesting history of thrift to be written based on non-Western thinking and practice.

The *Oxford English Dictionary* gives various definitions of the word thrift. The first, and oldest, describes it as a 'fact or condition of *thriving* [my italics] or prospering; prosperity, success, good luck'. The most recent explains thrift as 'economic management, economy, sparing us or expenditures of means, *frugality* [my italics], saving' – a meaning with which we are now more familiar. The word itself comes from the same root as thriving, but the emphasis has gradually been placed on management and frugality. From as early as the fourteenth century onwards, the meaning of thrift (as thriving) began to be distorted and utilised as part of various economic and theological discourses, and came to be understood as an economic and cultural practice based on frugality and frequently linked to respectability. In the nineteenth century, the British pastor and thrift advocate, William Blackley, described the change in the meaning of thrift from thriving and good fortune, to careful spending and providence', as a shift from an emphasis on the human condition, to the human character or 'habit' (1885). The choice of such words as character and habit was typical of an increasingly individualistic morality of the era that was quick to judge society's subjects, far less the mechanisms of state and society itself. (For example, Blackley's sentiments echo those of fellow Victorian Samuel Smiles.)

In fact, David Blankenhorn describes the 'gradual but steady evolution, largely completed by the mid nineteenth century' in how writers commonly used the word 'thrift', arguing that use of the word in its classical sense of growing and thriving increasingly gave way to referring to a set of habits and values, or character traits (Blankenhorn, 2008:19). Thrift, for many, stopped being an ethical discourse, and became a narrowly moral one (often prescribed by those in power). As Blankenhorn says, 'in brief, the word thrift is being gradually moralized … Instead of referring to life as a whole, life in all its flourishing … thrift in this new emphasis increasingly comes to mean first and foremost economic prosperity, or prosperity primarily in the material sense' (2008:19). Not by coincidence, this shift from one meaning to the other happened contemporaneously to changes in economic rationale and moral beliefs due to the increasing prominence of capitalism. In many ways this book, in attempting to analyse the relationship between capitalism and thrift, is precisely interested in an examination of this shift in meaning and the way in which thrift has been used by those with influence to enhance or rally against capitalism(s).

A by-product of this shift from thrift as thriving (ethical thrift), to thrift as frugality (moral thrift) is that (with a few exceptions) it has gradually been prised away from actually *belonging* to people as a practice of everyday life that can be used wilfully, tactically and sometimes as resistance. Instead, it has become rationalised as part of socio-economic arguments made by early capitalists, religious thinkers who tied their beliefs to capitalism and middle-class theorists. Thrift is a quintessentially bourgeois theory, which perhaps explains its status as a largely middle-class practice. After all, only those who have something to spare can practise thrift in its narrow economic sense.

However, thrift as thriving has refused to simply become a casualty of history as it were. The shift from ethical to moral thrift is not as all-encompassing or straightforward as some contemporary accounts might suggest. As what follows will show, it has its own history that has run parallel to, but not always referred to, or defined itself by, capitalism. In light of this, the utopian element towards the end of this book that attempts to re-cast thrift in more collective, economically egalitarian terms, also aspires to prise it away from the historical trajectory it has found itself part of, and reclaim it as a genuinely resistant practice.

Chapter 1 provides a discussion of some recent thinking on thrift in the academic world and attempts to begin to pick apart the ways in which thrift can and cannot be seen as part of, and helpful to, capitalisms across the globe. Chapter 2 looks at the beliefs of the early Puritans, Quakers and Methodists and the impact of religious thrift on social, economic and cultural attitudes and behaviour. Chapter 3 follows this by examining how Benjamin Franklin secularised the thrift of his forefathers, making it a specifically American value at the time, and how this had its European counterparts through Victorian moralism. In chapter 4 the spiritual, some would argue political, thrift of Henry Thoreau is posited as an antidote to Franklin and what came before, and his insistence on thrift as a sensuous practice is analysed. Chapter 5 looks at the nationalist flavour of thrift during the Second World War and afterwards and how today's policies often hark back to this era, romanticising it in the process. In chapter 6 we look at how thrift as a practice of saving money by not spending became about spending wisely and becoming a good consumer due to the influence of thinkers such as Keynes and the consumer rights movement of the early twentieth century onwards. Finally, in chapter 7 ecological thrift is explored, specifically contemporary concerns about the Anthropocene and the potential of de-growth as a practical and philosophical stance for tackling this challenge. The conclusion seeks to place thrift once again at the forefront of history and posit it as a genuinely resistant practice that seeks to question the logic behind much of the way society, certainly in the developed world, is run.

1

Towards a theory of thrift

Capitalism as the parasite of thrift

Mention thrift to most current-day academics in marketing, cultural studies or even cultural geography circles and one of the first theories they mention will be that of Daniel Miller in his *A Theory of Shopping* (2013). Using evidence from ethnographic research in north London, Miller argues that whilst shopping trips often begin by being about the pleasure of spending money, they frequently shift to focusing on saving money, and play upon traditional notions of restraint and sobriety being somehow more respectable than immediate gratification (Miller, 2013). Miller describes everyday shopping as containing two values – that of being thrifty ('saving' money), and that of expressing devotional love to significant others (spending). In doing so he adopts a dichotomous perspective of shopping as either provisioning or hedonic. Provisioning shopping is 'everyday', conducted out of necessity, and according to a utilitarian normative model in which individual desires are suppressed (2013). Whereas with hedonic shopping, goals are concerned with the satisfaction of particular individual desires, and the shopper regards it as an extravagance that lies outside the constraints of necessity.

For Miller, then, hedonic shopping is about self-indulgence and 'treat', whilst provisional shopping is concerned with thrift and short-term sacrifice in order to reach more substantial long-term goals, making it a more 'moral' act (2013).[1] Key to Miller's overall argument is the idea that thrift defers the 'treat' to a future moment and that this deferral is pleasurable for the shopper as part of sacrifice, in similar ways to which sacrifice is conceived of by anthropologists. In other words, essentially, this sacrifice is about love (in the widest sense). Miller argues its purpose 'is not so much to buy the things people want, but to strive to be in a relationship with subjects that want these things' (2013:148). (This could be rather neatly turned on its head in the case of thrift as thriving by formulating it thus – thrift is not so much about not buying the things people want, but about striving not to be in a relationship with subjects who want these things!)

Miller goes on to say that supermarket marketing strategies make thrift appear to be available everywhere, so that often shoppers need no price information to feel that they are practising thrift (2013:53). As Miller says, 'it is possible for shoppers to regard virtually the whole of the shopping expedition and the purchase of almost any specific item within that expedition, not as an act of spending at all, but as an act of saving' (2013:56). Such is the extent one might argue that capitalism has embedded itself in the idea and structures of thrift. Or, as Miller puts it later on, 'consumer thrift is now the centre piece of global economic ideology' (2013:136). (This also speaks rather nicely to the idea mentioned in the introduction that thrift is not in decline, but rather, is re-marketing itself as 'saving through spending' rather impressively!)

In contrast to Miller, in 'Thrift Shopping: Combining Utilitarian Thrift and Hedonic Treat Benefits', Fleura Bardhi and Eric Arnould propose a dialectical perspective of shopping that challenges Daniel Miller's positioning of thrift and treat as in opposition to one another (Bardhi and Arnould, 2005:223). They argue that the role of thrift can coexist with that of treat and that the related shopping practices are at once economic and hedonic, enabling consumers to negotiate and realise a diversity of moral and experiential experiences (2005:223). (This argument is also asserted by Sherry, 1990, and Falk and Campbell, 1997). Bardhi and Arnould's thrift shoppers 'understood and practiced thrift in coexistence with spending (shopping)' (2005:228), and can be contrasted to Lastovicka *et al.*'s 'frugal consumer' who understands being thrifty in terms of the sacrifice of present consumption for savings and a better future (1999). Bardhi and Arnould argue that thrift is not entirely about deferred gratification, as Miller suggests, because there is hedonic pleasure to be gained in thrift shopping that collapses the categories of thrift and treat (2005:228).

Bardhi and Arnould usefully challenge Miller's theory, allowing in the idea that thrift is often about the pleasure of a treat *in the present* through a thrifty purchase. This is an improvement on Miller's theory as it enables a conception of thrift whose logic is not some kind of future gratification. Viewed Miller's way, thrift remains bound within a normative economic framework in which the individual is posited as a kind of never-ending calculating machine, who walks around weighing up present sacrifice against future satisfaction as they shop. This individual is the one that most mainstream economic history is only too familiar with, Smith's 'economic man' who, through careful consideration of spending and saving, embodies consumerism and thrift and fuses them together in a symbiotic relationship (or perhaps more accurately, a parasitical one on the part of consumerism!). Bardhi and Arnould's shopper has rather more agency to portray themself as operating based on alternative logics of consumption, an important acknowledgement, and a theme to which this chapter will return in the following section.

Of course, Miller's shopper does exist too, or at least any shopper behaves like Miller's shopper at certain moments. It is the emphasis that mainstream economists and indeed mainstream renditions of economic history have placed on this economic man, whilst ignoring alternative versions, that is the issue here. In fact, the parasitical attachment of capitalism onto thrift, as embodied by Miller's shopper, has enabled the progress of capitalism across the centuries. This is to make a rather large statement, that, contrary to mainstream accounts in which thrift is seen as having faded away as capitalism grew stronger, only rearing its head at times of national crisis such as war or economic depression, *thrift has been a consistent undercurrent to capitalism.*

This mainstream portrayal of the history of thrift is captured well in Calder's critique of it. He complains that the view of history so frequently provided is one that portrays a slow decline from the morals and thrift of the early Puritans, to the wild consumerism of the present day – the story of American saving and spending as the story of a 'fall from the heights of thrift on which previous generations lived and contributed to national greatness' (2013:362). Despite basing his comments on the portrayal of American economic history, it can be applied more widely, as the same story is often told of the Western world more generally – economic history as a slow slide from thrift into spending. This is John Galbraith's view in his famous *The Affluent Society*; it is also apparent in David Tucker's *The Decline of Thrift in America*. Aligned to this is Daniel Bell's view in *The Cultural Contradictions of Capitalism* that the instalment plan and instant credit was the single major factor that destroyed the Protestant ethic. Similarly, Terrance Witkowski plots a history of frugality in the United States from the Puritan fathers to Voluntary Simplicity and up to the present, but essentially concludes that consumerism is the stronger historical strand and that consumers always returned to their previous habits. Calder calls these depictions of declining thrift 'the myth of lost economic virtue', but makes the point that it has not stood up well against more recent historical accounts that acknowledge contrary evidence and posit thrift as 'a surprisingly adaptable ethos operating across time and economic contexts' (2013:362). For Calder, thrift is dynamic and versatile.

This book argues that not only has there *not* been a slide from thrift to spending (at least not in a straightforward way), but that thrift has been a consistent underlying current in economic history, being practised, or at least preached, for various reasons throughout history. It has been present through good times and bad. In fact, capitalism could not have survived without thrift. Or rather, it could not have survived without *appropriating thrift as frugality* (whether that frugality was concerned with saving or spending).

Thrift as capitalism's Other

There is another side to this story of parasitical capitalism clinging to the thrift that keeps it functioning, however. Not all thrift can be put to the service of capitalism. Miller's shopper is not the only type of shopper. Economic man does not represent all people, all of the time, in fact he probably represents rather fewer people than mainstream economists might prefer to believe. Indeed, this book intends to debunk him as the assumed representative of all consumers, and provide another model, who is concerned not only with surviving through economic efficiency, but with *thriving* through economic, social and other forms of provisioning. This alternative human subject occupies a larger place in history than mainstream accounts have allowed for.

Whilst the survival of capitalism due to requisitioning thrift as frugality is crucial to acknowledge, as explained in the previous section, the contemporary scholar need not accept that capitalism has conquered thrift and that thrift must now only be seen as the handmaiden of capitalism. There are many historical 'moments', and indeed present practices of thrift, that successfully resist or hinder capitalism, despite its talent in re-appropriation. As Calder argues, if we can only see just how dynamic and versatile thrift has been throughout history then we can see how it does not only belong to 'Puritans and moralists, but also to peasants, monks, revolutionaries, conservationists, environmentalists, civil rights activists, philanthropists, social protestors, and others committed to an ethos of restraint' (2013:363–364). There is a clear alternative history of thrift that can be mapped philosophically as a strong lineage from Aristotle's notion of thriving, to Thomas Aquinas, to Marx, to Thoreau, and to present-day radical green movements. (This will be explored further in the conclusion.)

In order to release this alternative shopper, and alternative history, it is necessary to move beyond analysing thrift within the narrow constraints of the moment of exchange. Both Bardhi and Arnould, and Miller, remain fixed within the shopping 'moment' as it were, analysing thrift as part of a set of economic constraints and frameworks, as opposed to seeing it in wider terms. In fact, what is striking about Miller's theory of shopping, and the thoughts on thrift embedded within it, is not so much that the nature of thrift revolves around pleasure and sacrifice (which it certainly can do); but that Miller contextualises this within the narrow framework of shopping, as opposed to our everyday interactions with material things more generally. In doing so, he makes thrift something that is engaged in purely as part of economic transactions, thus trapping it within its more recent etymological definition – that of frugality. In fact, Miller's is a theory of frugality, not of thrift, and therefore disavows thrift of carving out a place for itself outside of mainstream capitalistic practices, or at the very least practices that aid capitalism.

David Evans makes a related argument, this time differentiating between thrift and frugality, but defining them both *within* the etymological definition of thrift understood as frugality. Like Miller, the result is that thrift is denied its sense of thriving. Evans' distinction between thrift and frugality is based on different 'scales of care and compassion that are mobilised through the (non)consumption practices associated with each' (2011:551). Referring to Miller's understanding of thrift as being about preserving household economic resources in order that they remain available for future acts of consumption that enable expressions of love and devotion, Evans defines thrift as 'the art of doing more (consumption) with less (money) and so thrifty practices are practices of savvy consumption, characterised by the thrill and skill of "the bargain"' (2011:551). He argues that 'thrift is essentially a circular process of spending to save and saving to spend. As such, it does not place a restraint on consumption, it merely seeks to save money whist doing so and then use monies saved to engage in further acts of consumption' (2011:552). This is a standard definition of thrift as it has come to be understood as frugality, although Evans does agree that, as a result, thrift can be understood as 'fully consummate with the prevailing logic of consumer cultures in which there is a normative surrounding high level of consumption' (2011:552).

Frustratingly, however, Evans then goes on to differentiate thrift from frugality, which he says has been under-theorised, and which he defines as the act of being 'moderate or sparing in the use of money, goods and resources with a particular emphasis on careful consumption and the avoidance of waste' (2011:552). For him, frugality is unlike thrift, because it is at odds with the normative expectations of consumer cultures. In reality, frugality, as it is understood by Evans, is only at odds with Keynesian logic, not with capitalism more generally. What he calls frugality is simply a different type of thrift, one that existed more commonly prior to consumer capitalism. In fact, in many ways what he makes is a false distinction between thrift (as wise shopping) and frugality; a distinction that only stands up when viewed in the context of relatively recent history, i.e. Keynes to the present and the onset of a specifically consumer capitalism. To put it differently, thrift for Evans is simply consumer thrift. Such definitions show how deep not only thrift as frugality, but thrift as consumer thrift, has embedded itself in the thinking around such issues.

Actually Evans' distinction between thrift and frugality (the latter often being ecological), is what this book posits as the difference between other forms of thrift and 'ecological thrift'. None of these forms of thrift when practised escape thrift as frugality, but ecological thrift is concerned with thriving in a far wider sense than simply economically. Evans even talks about there being parallels between ethics and morals, with thrift relating to morals (for example, the providing for our immediate family as a duty), and frugality relating to ethics (for example, the duty of care of distant others). In this, he draws again upon Miller, suggesting the same can be said for Miller's theory. This exact distinction between morals and ethics is the one this book makes between thrift (understood as frugality), and thrift (understood as thriving).

To be fair, neither Evans nor Miller were attempting a theory of thrift primarily, but this contextualising of the practice does mean historical reality is not well represented. Historically, people have engaged in thrift for all sorts of reasons – to get to heaven, to live a more fulfilling life, to challenge capitalism, to be respectable, to be part of a war effort. To assert frugality as a separate practice to thrift based on some greater ethical motivation is to cut off huge chunks of history and geography – practices of thrift as thriving at different times, in different places. Therefore, it is important to prise thrift away from the historical trajectory it has found itself part of, in order that it might be more easily claimed as a genuinely resistant practice, one that seeks to create collective and economically egalitarian forms of living that are available to all, not only those who can afford to choose them.

What stops this alternative history of thrift from rising immediately to the fore? Firstly, that it is based on thriving, when it is a history of frugality that dominates the currently accepted version of thrift's place in economic history. But, on a deeper level, it is the acceptance that it is capitalism and its 'spirit' that has been the main influence on economic history. (And actually, even Weber does not claim this, his only claim being that *Puritan* ethics aided a spirit of capitalism!) In this version of events, thrift serves capitalism, because it is assumed the major 'urge' is towards capitalistic ways of being.

There are two points to make in relation to this. Firstly, it should be acknowledged that there have been theories that play on the idea that it was a Puritan ethic that drove the spirit of capitalism. Notably Colin Campbell's well-known work *The Romantic Ethic and the Spirit of Modern Consumerism* (2005), which argues it has been romanticism, not Protestant rationality as Weber suggested, that has formed the backdrop for the capitalist spirit. Campbell sees this romanticism as linked to the rise of the idea of love as the ultimate emotion and reason for marriage, an increased secularity and the rise of fashion. This romantic thrust, according to Campbell, is what was behind the consumer revolution, not simply the urge to emulate, as Veblen argued. However, despite disagreeing on the driver of the spirit of consumerism/capitalism, Weber and Campbell both accept this spirit of capitalism as the only historical constant. One could, for example, equally argue that the romantic spirit could plausibly drive desires towards thrift in the form of alternative ways of thriving that provide more time or personal fulfilment. Indeed, one might re-name Thoreau's *Walden* as *The Romantic Ethic and the Spirit of Thrift!*

Secondly, to argue thrift as thriving is an urge *as strong as capitalism*, and indeed that works against capitalism and outside of capitalism, speaks to J. K. Gibson-Graham's calls not to posit capitalism as central – 'capitalocentrism' as they call it (2006).[2] This refers to the dominant representation of all economic activities in terms of their relationship to capitalism – as the same as, the opposite to, a complement of, or contained within capitalism. Gibson-Graham argue that capitalism is overdetermined and that there are many non-capitalist economic practices that exist alongside it. They explore alternative economic practices that they see as part of a 'politics of possibility', as part of an attempt to destabilise the hegemony of capitalocentrism by producing different representations of economic identity, and developing different narratives of economic development. This is not to fail to recognise capitalism's huge impact – capitalism has been incredibly successful at using thrift in its own interest. However, it has not managed to re-appropriate all thrifty beliefs or practices and the alternative history of thrift has not always defined itself simply in contrast to capitalism. Thrift as thriving is more than capable of creating itself without reference to the parameters of capitalism. The title of this section is in some ways misleading therefore, as thrift (as thriving) has been Othered by capitalism, rather than defining itself consistently as Other.

Arguments such as these are captured in current-day discourses on post-development and de-growth, which will be explored in more depth in the final chapter in the context of ecological imperative. For now, suffice to say that both de-growth and post-development are concerned with removing themselves completely from the logic of growth as necessity and of any imagination of a linear trajectory from 'developing' or 'underdeveloped' to 'developed'. As

Demaria and Kothari rightly insist, 'these worldviews are not a novelty of the twenty-first century, but they are rather part of a long search for and practice of alternative ways of living' (2017:2592).

Scarcity, abundance and morality

Alongside the established narrative in which thrift slides into consumerism is the equally established and related narrative in which an age of scarcity gives way to an age of abundance. This asserts that the consumer revolution came about as a result of increased production due to industrialisation and the mechanisation it entailed, alongside increased demand for the products produced created by advertising and the Veblen-esque desire of lower social classes to emulate higher ones. These two phenomena are now broadly accepted to require one another if they are to explain the consumer revolution – rising availability of goods and rising ability to pay for them alone is no longer considered a viable explanation without the important addition of attitudinal change.

Most famously, Neil McKendrick *et al.* (1984:11) assert that social emulation was the key motive for the increased propensity to consume which was an essential factor in the Industrial (and therefore consumer) Revolution. For McKendrick *et al.*, then, Veblen's conspicuous consumption was the major driver in the consumer revolution and it was therefore the rich who led the revolution as their spending provoked the consumer desire of the middle classes, and theirs in turn that of the lower classes. For McKendrick *et al.*, social emulation saw the pursuit of luxuries rather than 'decencies', and decencies rather than necessities (1984:98). They attribute this emulation to the onset of fashion in the middle of the eighteenth century and the speed with which trends suddenly started changing with regularity when previously they had remained stable for long periods. This narrative tends to portray the 1920s as the watershed moment when the 'nineteenth century "producer ethic" – an ethos of restraint, thrift, and work, arising from conditions of scarcity – was surpassed by a twentieth century "consumer ethic" that took abundance for granted and found expression in lifestyles of release, therapeutic indulgence, and fun' (Calder, 2013:357).

Working alongside this 'myth of lost economic virtue', as mentioned in the previous section and typified by the work of Galbraith, Tucker and Bell who insist on a slide from frugality to spending, is a normative economic history that posits a shift from scarcity to abundance. This shift is typified by Simon Patten's argument that America went from being a society of scarcity to one of abundance, David

Potter's insistence that American history and its 'national character' emerged from an economy of abundance (1954), and again John Kenneth Galbraith's famous warning that the vociferous chasing of private wealth was based specifically upon the premise of an *affluent* society (1958). All these accounts, despite coming from very different positions, posit a tide of abundance against which moral rights and wrongs are carried out. Firstly, this not the case in any simplistic way, as abundance has proved a most uneven and discriminatory tide, which creates pockets of wealth and vast swaths of deprivation even in developed countries. Abundance is not neutral. Economic polarisation is rife. Even when abundance is most present, not everyone has access to it, and certainly not under equal terms. For many, it is unobtainable abundance on the whole. Secondly, and more frustratingly, this positing of an age of abundance means anyone arguing that in reality thrift is just as easily evidenced historical backdrop, can be accused of not sufficiently recognising the impact of capitalism.

This book, then, has the difficult task of attempting to fully recognise capitalism whilst insisting that social history, even in the developed West, displays thriving and frugality as consistently present phenomena for a variety of reasons. In fact, capitalism's presence is clear, but its constant attempts to install a thrift that serves its own purposes, as opposed to one that seeks out ways of skirting around capitalism's rules and machinations, are what is interesting. And alongside this, the successes of thrift, in the sense of thriving, to plough its own historical furrow despite this.

The positing of history as a slide into degenerate spending due to an era of abundance unfortunately also enables the promotion of thrift as frugality on decidedly moral grounds. Of course, consumption has always been tied up with morals, as the case studies in this book show only too clearly, but thrift as thriving has the ability to promote an ethics for living as opposed to a more righteous kind of morality. This righteous morality can come from the political Right and Left; for example, it can be puritanical (Right), or it can be the anti-capitalist morals of the Frankfurt School and its current-day equivalents (Left). Briefly, this latter can be seen as beginning with Veblen and his insistence that consumption is motivated by false and shallow values, leading to wasteful and extravagant consumption that diverts capital from 'useful' ends. It was then taken up by Frankfurt School theorists such as Walter Benjamin and Theodor Adorno, and influenced Baudrillard and more recent scholars. One constant theme is that the desire for commodities is about the pressures of modernity and some kind of malaise within society itself, i.e. that consuming is some form of 'medicine' for human subjects struggling to live in current times. This stance, broadly speaking, comes from cultural elites who blame the 'fakeness' of mass culture, but also from liberals who see it as symptomatic of the alienating nature of consumer capitalism, and indeed capitalism more generally.

As Wilk argues, moral debate about consumption is an essential and ancient part of human politics, and an inevitable consequence of the unique way human relationships with the material world have developed. Therefore, 'there is no question that moralizing about consumption can be strategically deployed during class conflict, inter-ethnic strife, nationalist or fundamentalist agitation, religious anti-secularism, and even trade negotiations' (2001:246). As McKendrick *et al.* point out, academics are all too easily unwitting accomplices in this ideological warfare, and need to be more aware of the ways in which this happens in order to better resist it (McKendrick *et al.*, 1984). For many academics, this has meant a backlash against Frankfurt School fears about 'false needs' and 'manufactured desires', and a rebellion in the form of an acceptance of consumerism, or even a positing of consumerism as about choice and agency. Such backlash forgets the extent to which structures curtail people's buying and indeed non-buying habits and can easily fall into the trap of treating consuming as an equivalent to voting.

Wilk's position provides a useful middle ground; or rather, is usefully different to both the spending-as-evil and spending-as-agency arguments. Rather than condemning the moral thread, he suggests that consumption is in essence a moral matter, 'since it always and inevitably raises issues of fairness, self versus group interests, and immediate versus delayed gratification' (2001:246). So, whilst recognising the worst aspects of morality on consumption, he also makes a case for maintaining morals, specifically in light of consumption practices that are 'socially, ecologically and personally destructive' (2001:246). Usefully distinguishing between the economic aspects and the failure to acknowledge agency in the work of Marx, Wilk argues that Marx's critique of consumer capitalism falls within the same moralistic tradition of social self-criticism, and that the concept of commodity fetishism causes us to disregard what people have to say about their own consumption and view all their desires as somehow 'false' (2001:248). However, importantly, he goes on to say that Marx's rationale is preferable to Veblen's or Freud's, because he sees the desire for commodities as part of an economic system which exploits some and rewards others: 'Marx's moralism was therefore essentially political rather than social (Veblen) or personal (Freud)' (2001:248).

All such moral positions on consumption, and indeed thrift, arise from the apparent age of abundance experienced in the developed parts of the world. Yet the same kind of Left-wing moral logic is applied by some thinkers to the developing world. Jean-Marc Philibert's work is a classic example of this. Philibert argues that consumption in the developing world is part of the impact of neo-colonialism due to the way in which cheap copies displace local culture, convincing those who buy them that they will attain modernity and sophistication in doing so (Philibert, 1990). For Philibert, then, developing world consumers can only ever purchase things in order to try (and fail) to aspire to some kind of norm or quality created by developed countries. In contrast, Wilk insists on consumers' (including those in the developing world) ability to make creative, resistant and expressive choices, but also recognises that consumption that enters new markets from developed markets can of course be highly exploitative – 'Within every developing country there are groups that are particularly vulnerable to addictive and exploitative forms of consumption' (Wilk, 2001:252). He goes on to cite, as examples, the many historical cases where alcohol or drugs have played a role in destroying communities (2001:252).[3]

Certainly, it is the case that local re-appropriations of products occur all the time; what is more concerning here is that the unquestioned acceptance of abundance causes moral judgement not only on those who consume in the developed world, but on those in the developing world too! Berating 'mistaken' notions of what commodities can do for one's happiness is most certainly not the answer. This book is about berating the system that causes commodities to often appear as, or indeed actually be, the best answer.

2

Religious thrift: Puritans, Quakers and Methodists

Puritans and predestination

The 'frugality' definition of thrift as 'economic management, economy, sparing us or expenditures of means, frugality, saving' is the one with which we are now most familiar. This second meaning, according to Yates and Hunter, did not emerge until around 200 years after the first. They argue that up until the fourteenth century, thrift did not exist 'as a category of moral reflection or practical ethics'; rather, thrift in the sense of frugality emerged with the transformation of economies in Europe between the fourteenth and sixteenth centuries. During this time, money, as opposed to barter, gradually became the founding force of economies (2011:8). This period culminated in the Puritan[1] beliefs of the seventeenth century (2011:8), so it was with the early Puritans that the oldest etymological sense of thrift – that of thriving, gave way to the more recent version – that of frugality. Consequently, the Puritans and their beliefs are crucial for any exploration into the concept of thrift and its present-day applications.

The Puritans gained their name due to their desire to 'purify' the Church of England from all Roman Catholic elements; they advocated greater purity of worship and doctrine, alongside personal and collective piety. This meant moral purity must be pursued to the smallest detail – man existed for the glory of God and above all else must do God's will, including in the economic realm. Not surprisingly, this pursuing of purity led to an extreme asceticism, and a reputation for eradicating any form of pleasure. This reputation was not without evidence as once they had legislative power Puritans in England banned social occasions that were seen as part of 'merry England', such as Whitsun Ales, May Day celebrations, theatre and Christmas (Roberts, 2015). In addition of course, such pleasure-denying appears in the writings of Puritans themselves – Cotton Mather was famously against dancing, insisting that each step of it brought one closer to hell (Mather, 1692: 16–17). Such connotations were not aided by H. L.

Mencken's famous declaration that Puritanism could be defined as 'the haunting fear that someone, somewhere, may be happy' (2015). Puritanism, in the popular imagination at least, has gone way beyond thrift!

However, as Stephen Roberts points out, this is a stereotype that is worth some questioning. Many historical experts have found evidence that suggests a more nuanced relationship with pleasure; one that emphasised appropriateness rather than disallowing pleasure altogether (see, for example, Miller, 1939; Daniels, 1995; McKay, 2008). Roberts himself draws upon the work of the Puritan, Ralph Venning, in his assertion that the pursuit of happiness played a key role in Puritan thought. He points to the strong influence of Aristotle on Venning and other Puritans such as John Goodwin (Roberts, 2015:183). What is more certain, is the presence of a background anxiety as characteristic of the Puritan experience of inner life. Both R. T. Kendall and Joel Beeke suggest that this anxiety was rooted in Puritanism's emphasis on predestination. Darren Oldbridge goes further, arguing that Puritan preaching basically taught the bleak message that the joys of salvation were unobtainable without suffering and pain. Meanwhile, John Stachniewski asserts that the relationship between Puritan theology and the economic and social context of the time led to the promotion of a religion of despair (1991). Indeed, it is with the economic considerations, as opposed to the atmosphere of asceticism, that it becomes easier to understand the all-prevailing presence of thrift in Puritan thinking and living.

Puritan economic ethics were born of a powerful combination of individual moral striving and a collective project of mutual aid and social reform, backed by a robust religious and civil institutional context – not least the thinking of Calvin and to a lesser extent Luther (Yates and Hunter, 2011:9). A basic tenet of Puritan economic thrift was that of charity. As Eaton argues, the Puritan line was that one should not loan to another who is in need; rather one should give alms. If one must loan to another who is in need, repayment should not be expected – the welfare of others was always more important than one's own (Eaton, 2013:7). In this instance Puritan thinking was more akin to the Lutheran view than the Calvinist one, Calvin being in some ways highly pragmatic when faced with the economic realities of his native Switzerland. Luther saw interest-bearing loans of any type as an attempt to gain from the labour and/or misfortune of others and therefore as a manifestation of greed. He advocated giving alms or lending with no expectation of return (Luther, 2013). Calvin, in marked contrast, both to Luther and to the church's tendency to condemn lending based on the prohibition in Deuteronomy (23:19–20), constructed a theological defence of some forms of interest taking, making a distinction between borrowing money due to economic need and borrowing money for profit-making purposes (Eaton, 2013:1).

However, it was the belief in predestination that is the key to understanding how Puritan economic morality led to the emphasis on thrift as frugality – the aspect of Puritan faith that has now become the main association, with 'puritanism' even being used as an antonym of hedonism. (This aspect was, of course, emphasised by Weber in his famous work on the Protestant work ethic, but was also brought into popular understanding by Benjamin Franklin's later form of Puritanism that will be explored in the following section.) Doing God's will (and therefore proving that one was predestined for Heaven) was best evidenced by the manifestation of 'good works'. Importantly, these came to include one's means of making a living, as Puritan belief saw work as one's 'calling' from God to serve Him by serving the community – an idea heavily influenced by Calvinist thought. In Book III of the *Institutes* Calvin writes that 'the Lord bids each one of us in all life's actions to look to his calling' and that 'each individual has his own kind of living assigned to him by the Lord as a sort of sentry post so that he may not heedlessly wander about throughout life' (Calvin, 2007:99). For Calvin, then, as for the Puritans, our calling in life has been predestined by God. Furthermore, callings are about interdependence, as the 'fact that one has a particular calling requires an individual to depend on others who have different callings' (Eaton, 2013:5).

It was Luther who had set the thinking for this belief by reforming the view of work, making a 'calling' (*beruf*) secular work as well as church work. Previously, there had been what Bonhoeffer (1959) refers to as a two-tiered Christianity, with some 'called' into church-related vocations, and less committed others living out Christian lives in the secular realm. In his *To the Christian Nobility* Luther dismissed this separation and advocated for all workers to see their labour as a calling from God and therefore pleasing to Him. In fact, Bainton (1950) argues that Luther unwittingly aided the development of capitalism in this way, despite his opposition to it. In *Trade and Usury* (1524) Luther advocates commerce only for the exchange of necessities. He argues that international trade is 'ostentation' and drains money from the people; merchants are sinners as they are avaricious. Luther challenges the idea that the merchant may sell goods for the highest price possible, arguing that to sell one's goods for the highest possible price shows no regard for one's neighbour, especially as the more desperate the buyer is for the good being sold, the higher the price that can be commanded for that good. For Luther, price should reflect only the cost of making the good and the labour, time and risk of the merchant. He is also against asking different prices for cash and credit buyers, and robustly condemns monopolists who control the market. It is the role of government, he argues, to oversee the market and fix prices when needed to ensure that justice and equity rule in the economy.

Such ideas were in striking contrast to previous ideas of work as toil that would hinder a Christian life. One could now apply oneself to a vocation and still view life as a service to God. Luther, Calvin and the Puritans had made work honourable as a service to God, enabling people to work with enthusiasm and without shame. As Eaton asserts, Calvin took issue with the Catholic teaching that the contemplative life is to be preferred over the life of toil, a teaching that had come from the story of Mary and Martha, where Mary was commended for listening to Jesus as opposed to working. Calvin held that the problem was not that Martha was working, but that she was working at a time when she should not have been (Eaton, 2013:6). For Calvin, then, money-making need not be considered socially degrading and morally dangerous, as it had previously. Calvin also viewed all types of work as equal, if for no other reason than it is the offering of the labourer to God. Unlike Luther, he saw usefulness in trade and commerce, in the context of community benefits (Calvin, 2007).

The Puritan attitude towards work (as God's work) was, however, one of precise ethical balance; a balance based on one hand on resisting greed and on the other on being respectful and careful with wealth. The reasoning was that financial rewards were likely to follow diligent work (and Calvin too had seen prosperity as God's blessing), but that this could create a temptation to work for financial gain as opposed to for God. Wealth accumulation as motivation for work was against Puritan ethics. Yet wealth accumulation as a by-product of undertaking God's calling of work was ethically sound as long as it was not spent in a wanton manner. As Eaton says, 'wealth that was earned was not to be spent, but to be used to further one's own calling or used for the benefit of others' – an approach that rewards faithful service within one's calling and urges thrift and frugality with the rewards (Eaton, 2013:8). Importantly, then, thrift for the Puritans was not an individual private matter, but a spiritual calling for whole communities. We really were then, at least to some extent, 'all in it together' as far as Puritans were concerned. Indeed, Puritans believed thrift to be a necessary condition for human thriving as it was the correct response to divine grace. However, it was also an ethic of responsible, profitable and pious management of time and talents and *any material things* that came from them (Davis and Mathewes, 2011) and it was in this way that thrift as frugality became highly prized amongst Puritans.

This combination of hard work and careful use of resources, especially in the form of strong capital that could then be invested in future productive activities, has of course been recognised (by Weber and many others) as attitudes most useful for the quick expansion of a capitalist system. For Weber, in his attempt to explain what he saw as a new spirit that fostered capitalism, this Puritan/Calvinist strain provided a ready answer (Weber, 1992). But whilst Puritan beliefs could be said to support a competitive market, they did not support an *unfettered* market, robustly condemning unbridled capitalism, gain for the sake of gain, or gain at the expense of others. As had Calvin before them, Puritans believed in the regulation of markets at certain times, in order to prevent human greed and make it more likely that market outcomes worked for all. Through the influence of Calvin, they also believed in self-denial and putting the interests of others first. These two central tenets can be neatly witnessed in book 3 of Calvin's *Institutes* where he writes, 'when Scripture tells us not to put aside selfish interests, it not only removes undue desire for wealth, power or popularity from our minds, but wipes out all ambitions for worldly glory' (2007:III. vii. and 2).

By the seventeenth century Puritan religious beliefs had taken root, having huge cultural effects in England and Scotland, as well as in the United States following 1630, when many Puritans left for New England in order to support the founding of the Massachusetts Bay Colony and various other settlements. In these areas, Puritan hegemony lasted for at least a century, with key figures emerging as the leaders of specific generations – John Cotton and Richard Mather (1630–1661) from the founding to the Restoration; Increase Mather (1662–1689) from the Restoration and the Halfway Covenant to the Glorious Revolution; Cotton Mather (1689–1728) from the new charter until his death (Carpenter, 2003:41). The faithful were encouraged to strive for profit in the name of undertaking God's calling; to avoid debt and lending; and to manage resources carefully and live frugally. Whilst Weber's understanding of these as the perfect conditions for capitalism still stands, such factors can also be seen as the perfect conditions for thrift. After all, more profit emerges not only from making more money, but also from having fewer costs. It is perhaps more accurate to argue, as Eaton does, that whilst Puritan beliefs were arguably a long way from a 'capitalist spirit', their manifestation certainly provided a ripe context for the development of capitalist structures. As a result, thrift as frugality emerges as tied into the history of capitalism from the very early stages of its development, even via the ethics of those who were not natural friends of all-out capitalism (such as Calvin).

Under Puritan thought, Smith's 'economic man' was not yet an independent economic unit, and could (and should) only be understood in relation to his fellow economic men. What is interesting here is whether the Puritans saw this spiritual calling for collective responsibility as one that required the faithful to go against their sinful, but perhaps 'natural', desire to be selfish, or whether they were early subscribers to an alternative notion to that of Smith's – reciprocal man. Reciprocal man is best understood as the opposite of the more well-known economic man – that is an individual who is defined by self-interest and therefore attempts to maximise utility and profit for themselves only for the least possible effort put in.[2] In contrast, reciprocal man is primarily motivated by the desire to cooperate and improve the wider environment, as opposed to being focused solely on his own conditions. The distinction here is an important one as it determines whether the puritanical attitude towards human nature (i.e. self-interested or community-interested) means their thrift was essentially one which saw money as evil, or one which saw it as the least harmful of various evils and which could therefore be used for greater good. History presents the answer as the latter if we accept that puritanical doctrine came via Calvin and therefore via Augustine, as Augustine's thought most certainly fed into that which saw the State as responsible for holding back the worst of the 'passions', including greed, and making something useful of them.

Briefly, as Hirschman's (1977) excellent account attests, money-making became honourable when a few strands of religious and political thinking broke away from the church's established use of Thomas Aquinas' thought which scorned material acquisition, and attempted to make it acceptable by separating the 'interests' from the 'passions'. Augustine's thought was key to this new interpretation as he differentiated between the love of glory, which he saw as able to have redeeming social value, and the purely private pursuit of riches. For Augustine, it was the State that must be the mechanism for holding back the worst passions and harnessing them in the name of 'interests'.

Later, as Hirschman argues, both repression of the passions, and harnessing 'interests' to overcome them, seemed to lack persuasiveness, so a third solution, to discriminate amongst the passions and use the apparently more innocuous passions to counteract a more dangerous and destructive set, emerged as the answer (1977:20). As 'danger' was seen as embodied in lust more than in any other passion, avarice was left free to emerge as the less frightful passion that could be deployed in the attempt to maintain the calm of the others. So, the scene was already set for Montesquieu to take this strand of thinking one step further, and argue that not only could avarice be used for 'good', but that even when not being 'harnessed' in the name of that project, it could unwittingly conspire towards the public good (2002). This 'invisible hand' meant the role of the state in repressing passions was now far less necessary, if not totally unnecessary. Montesquieu's argument went on to suggest that not only could self-interest lead to betterment for all, but that the trade which emerged from this self-interested desire, by necessity, 'polished' and 'softened' barbarian ways due to a mutual dependence (2002:80). By creating a strong web of interdependent relationships, it was thought, domestic trade would create more cohesive communities, and foreign trade would help avoid wars between countries. This 'doux commerce' can be directly compared to Smith's 'many advantages' arising from man's 'natural desire' to barter (2003).

This was clearly a break from Aquinas' view which had previously dominated and which Hirschman (1977) traces back to Aristotle, arguing that it manifests itself as a general condemnation of money and trade, along with a celebration of self-sufficiency and production for use. In *Politics* (2009), Aristotle defines man's wants as naturally finite, and, therefore, trade as only natural in that it restores self-sufficiency as we exchange what we do not need for what we do: 'Interchange of this kind is not contrary to nature and is not a form of money-making; it keeps to its original purpose – to re-establish nature's own equilibrium of self-sufficiency' (2009:42). (Note that many of these themes resonate with the original definition of thrift as thriving mentioned in the introduction to this book.) Self-sufficiency, for Aristotle, required reciprocity, which was natural and therefore good; profit-oriented exchange was deemed unnatural and destructive of the bonds between people and households. The Aristotelian theme that has carried through epistemologically is that of trading 'for the sake of', becoming trading 'for its own sake', the transition from one to the other being a moral mistake according to Aristotle. It was in the thirteenth century that Aristotle's ideas were taken up by Thomas Aquinas and the church authorities who saw many evils in material acquisition, such as the idea that merchants did not 'produce' anything, so they did not 'work' yet still earned from the labourer. It is because of Aquinas' preoccupation with material production that Marx's labour theory of value is often viewed as the last in a long line from Aristotle.

So, whilst one historical strand saw money as demoralising, alienating, corrupting and destructive of community, the other culminated in the view of money as a great force for betterment and 'civilisation'. Strangely then, despite their asceticism, the ethics of the Puritans fell into the latter camp and can perhaps help explain the seemingly paradoxical outcome of Puritan thrift – that is the way in which a deeply pious attitude towards accumulation of material things led to a highly effective technique for material accumulation. Considering also how this historical strand developed, culminating in the highly individualistic and laissez-faire economics of thinkers such as Hayek, it is perhaps not surprising that the original collective aspect of Puritan thrift began to give way to a much more individualistic conception of it by the end of the Puritan era – the late seventeenth century. Indeed, as Yates and Hunter argue, in the post-Puritan eighteenth century, thrift was 'more narrowly economic and private in focus than the Puritan vision' and came with 'a clear duty towards charity and benevolence, but one that was more concerned with personal propriety and individual material well-being' (2011:20).

Quakers and utilitarian frugality

The Puritan vision of frugality, however, was not the only one available in the seventeenth century. The Quaker movement, with its emphasis on plain living and thrift, looked very similar to Puritan thought at first glance, but the two movements could not have been more opposed.[3] Quakerism was begun in England by George Fox, whose key belief was that 'Christ has come to teach his people himself', meaning believers had a personal and *direct* relationship with God and did not require intermediaries (Fox, 1803:186).[4] The eradicating of a fearsome and powerful God was disturbing enough, but the greatest threat to the Puritans was that the Quakers did not believe in the Calvinist doctrine of predestination, and in doing so 'raised the spectre of antinomian individualism and religious toleration' (Shi, 2007:28). This lack of absolute 'laws' governing religious belief, and the Quaker insistence upon a form of relativism, coupled with their devotion to individualism, pacifism and egalitarianism, caused them to be seen as extreme Left-wingers by the Puritans – even anarchists. So much so in fact, that Quakers were persecuted, tortured and hung by Puritans in the early days of the Massachusetts colony. Indeed, the establishment of Pennsylvania by the Quaker William Penn was in large part to provide a safe haven for persecuted Quakers (Baltzell, 1996:86).[5]

Yet, despite their fundamental differences, the Quaker message appeared, in practice, to echo Calvin in a firm belief in the virtues of thrift, sobriety and hard work at one's calling. Quakers were not against riches, but were wary of them, believing it was preferable and correct to keep oneself free of such concerns in order to be able to live without having to constantly consider material possessions. As George Fox said, 'neither be cumbred nor surfeited with the riches of this world, nor bound, nor strained with them' (Fox, 1803:198). Or, in the words of William Penn, 'riches serve wise men, but command a fool' (Penn, 2016:83). Another early Quaker, Robert Barclay, spoke of the necessity to base riches on needs not desires. In addition, the 'Testimony of Simplicity' meant that Quakers also believed in simple dress and manners, without the use of titles. This testimony, although a result of changed times, remains central to Quaker practice today.[6]

However, it is important to note that there was, from the outset, a political dimension to Quaker thought; for them, living simply would not simply counter greed (as it would for the Puritans), it would also promote social justice and create a more egalitarian society. Like so much of Quaker thought it was concerned with making improvement in this world, not guaranteeing a future in another one. Sharing wealth was key to Quakers, who insisted that the widening gap between rich and poor should be narrowed and that wealth should benefit the community as a whole (Davies, 2000:273). Penn himself saw thrift as guarding against decline in society, believing through his study of history that when luxury became prevalent in societies they declined. Penn involved a strain of localism in this thinking too, however, believing that thrift and frugality would enable society to provide for itself and not have to rely upon foreign trade. This should, though, be viewed in the context of the times, in which debt was rife, and fear of owing debt to foreign merchants was understandably an influence, as opposed to being seen as a philosophical belief in self-sufficiency for its own sake.

This belief in wealth-sharing is reflected in the current-day economic practices of Quakers including the 'Quakernomics' of companies such as John Lewis which attempt to avoid huge disparities in pay between employees at different levels and enable all employees to benefit from the company's profits.[7] In fact, Quaker thrift is perhaps the closest any thrift comes to being genuinely collective. Furthermore, the return for the endeavour of thrift was seen as being important in 'this life', in the here and now, not as a way of guaranteeing a place in heaven, largely because, for Quakers, God was not an all-powerful external entity, but resided within oneself. Put this way, it becomes clearer quite why the Quaker religious beliefs were so threatening to the Puritans.

Interestingly, the Quakers were initially better than the Puritans at maintaining this belief in simple living and thrift, and did remain less materialistic, despite their impressive ability to generate wealth. Shi puts this down to the Quaker ethic being designed to teach Quakers how to live, rather than how to make a living (2007:29). In many ways, Quaker thinking, then and now, is the closest to a notion of thrift as thriving (and collective thriving specifically). It certainly sits a long way from thrift as economic frugality pure and simple, or for its own sake. As Michaelis argues, many Quakers lived more simply than non-Quakers at their level of income, and due to the collective nature of their thrift, as a community they were very well off (2008:99). The less positive side of this was that there was an insular nature to Quakers at this time – partly as they had been forced to set up their own businesses due to persecution and wanted to conduct business by their own ethics and rules, but partly because they did not want their wealth to leave the community. 'Marrying out' caused Quakers to be disowned by their communities in many cases (see Michaelis, 2008:99).

However, eventually Quakers, like their Puritan contemporaries, began to make and enjoy their fortunes and move to cities, despite Penn himself encouraging people to be 'plain farmers', and advocating a country life as being more in touch with God. Penn's words had perhaps lost some of their power, not least because he himself lived in splendour, with his own vineyards and horses, a large coterie of staff, and fine goods ordered from across the globe for him to consume and enjoy. As Shi argues, 'for the masses he advised austerity; for himself and a few others like him, he supported enlightened gentility' (2007:36). Essentially, like Benjamin Franklin after him, Penn was a hypocrite, only partially getting away with this contradiction due to the way in which many rich Quakers saw no contradiction because temperance was a virtue *relative to* one's social standing. Quite how this social standing could be explained in light of Quaker principles towards a more equal society remains an unanswered question.

It is worth mentioning that in the 1740s, with the 'Great Awakening', many Quakers returned to their thrifty roots, influenced by those such as John Fothergill, Anthony Benezet and John Woolman – who was to prove a great inspiration to Samuel Taylor Coleridge.[8] However, for most, frugality was not the focus, and indeed only really reoccurred in the early twentieth century when concerns were voiced at the annual meeting in London about the levels of consumption in modern life (Michaelis, 2008:101). Since then, Quaker thrift has often been oriented around ethical consumption and responsible ecological behaviour, and is often these beliefs that the 'testimony of simplicity' taps into today. Coleman and Collins found Quaker members to be familiar with parts of *Quaker Faith and Practice* such as 'Try to live simply. A simple lifestyle freely chosen is a source of strength. Do not be persuaded into buying what you do not need or cannot afford' (*Quaker Faith and Practice*, 1995:para. 1.02, quoted in Coleman and Collins, 2000:323). Quakers have also pioneered collective living environments that uphold these principles, effectively living out a version of thrift that most closely resonates with thrift as thriving, not frugality.

John Wesley and Methodist thrift

It would not be possible to write a chapter on religious thrift without acknowledging the contribution of the founder of the Methodist church – John Wesley (1703–1791), and to a lesser extent his younger brother Charles Wesley (1707–1788). More pertinently, it is important to acknowledge the ways in which Methodism differed from Puritanism, despite a mutual belief in the power of a relatively austere life, and the impact this had, and indeed still has, on the practice of thrift.

Methodism began as a movement within the Church of England due to the Wesley brothers' founding of the 'Holy Club' at Lincoln College, University of Oxford. The club practised fasting, abstaining from most forms of amusement, refusing luxury, and spent much time visiting the poor, the sick and prisoners. The word 'Methodist' was initially a term of insult used by their peers at Oxford who saw their religious lives as governed by rule and method (Frazer, 2015). In 1735, both John and Charles Wesley were invited by the founder of the Georgia colony in America to be ministers. The mission failed, and they returned to England where they preached to individuals and groups in houses, religious societies and a few churches, as well as fields, collieries and churchyards (Frazer, 2015). In fact, Methodist lay preachers appointed by the Wesleys particularly focused on potential converts who they felt had been neglected by the Church of England and who often did not attend church (Hylson-Smith, 1992:17–21).

Crucially, it was at this time that John Wesley was highly influenced by the work of Jacobus Arminius (1560–1609), a Dutch theologian who had rejected the Calvinist idea that only a preordained group of people would find their way into heaven.[9] Wesley quickly became an outspoken opponent of the doctrine of predestination; a fearless anti-Calvinist who insisted salvation was available to all. Perhaps as a result, early Methodists came from all classes within society. Indeed, in Britain, the relationship between Methodism and the development of the working class as a conscious political entity is an intricate one. This is proven not least by the argument within and subsequent reactions to E. P. Thompson's *The Making of the English Working Class*.[10] In the United States, it is perhaps slightly more straightforward. Due to its missions, but also its championing of the rights of slaves, Methodism became the religion of many slaves and former slaves. Also, as Richard Carwardine points out, for many working-class people in America, Methodism (and Baptism) were part of a movement to mobilise against the new economic order that occurred alongside subsistence farming and workers' movements (2001). This gave Methodism the reputation of being a 'parochial' religion.

The idea that anyone could find their way to heaven through hard work and charity not surprisingly held mass appeal. Thrift, as a way to get into heaven, not simply a way to *maintain one's place* in heaven, was once again a strong presence. Accordingly, like the Puritans and Quakers before them, early Methodists wore plain clothes and condemned ornamentation such as ruffles, laces, gold or anything that was, or was supposed to look, costly (Lyerly, 1998:39). In his sermon, 'On Dress', Wesley famously said, 'Let me see, before I die, a Methodist congregation, full as plain dressed as a Quaker congregation' (Ehrman, 2003). Also like Quakers, Methodists did not participate in gambling of any kind, nor did they go to the theatre or dances, or drink alcohol.

John Templeton interprets Wesley's promotion of thrift through the Parable of the Talents.[11] Briefly, the parable tells the tale of a man who is going on a journey and chooses three servants to look after his resources whilst he is away. He gives the first servant five talents (coins), the second servant two talents, and the third servant just one talent. The first servant puts the talents to immediate good use and turns the five talents into ten. The second servant has similar success, also doubling his talents and turning two into four. The third servant simply digs a hole and buries his talent. The man is pleased with the first two talents and rewards the first by giving the coin entrusted to the third servant to him. According to Templeton, whilst this reaction to the third servant might seem harsh, the parable is essentially about stewardship and what we *do* with what we are given. For Templeton, thrift is not simply about spending or doing less, but about actively using what we have wisely. Therefore, the third servant did not practise thrift as he simply did nothing with his coin; his actions are equated to 'being lazy' or expecting to get 'something for nothing' (2011:15). This specifically Methodist take on thrift is based on the idea that we can all potentially earn a place in heaven through our careful stewardship whilst on earth and sits in direct contrast to the Puritan idea that we have a preordained place in heaven that we can only *lose* through bad behaviour.

For Templeton, thrift is equated to financial wisdom – 'In considering how they will use their resources, thrifty people are committed to making careful, thoughtful decisions. This does not make them cheap; it makes them wise' (2011:17). This is a sadly narrow definition of thrift, that purports to be far removed from Calvinist motivations, but in practice is not, and does little to challenge those Calvinistic urges to behave correctly as part of a life based essentially on 'the market'. It seems more suited to a Weberian interpretation of Christian thought, than a Methodist one (apparently based on spiritual fulfilment rather than financial gain). One might ask, what if the third servant did not expect or want any more, and just wanted to keep his coin safe and spend his time concentrating on less commercial activities? Might it not be acceptable to engage in a thrift that was about needing less (and therefore not making profit), if that meant more time was available to do what was important to ourselves and others? In fact, Templeton's alignment of thrift with financial wisdom typifies the morally righteous ideologies behind financial education in schools in the United States – teachings that many might validly argue simply taught young people to be good capitalists. Indeed, Templeton's interpretation does not posit thrift as in any way outside of, or potentially outside of, mainstream capitalist economic thought.

This is not quite so of Wesley himself, whose message and indeed life practice were slightly more at odds with capitalism pure and simple. Wesley's take on thrift was very specific, and can best be captured by analysing his now-famous sermon on 'The Uses of Money', which forms the basis of the Methodist attitude towards money then and indeed in the present day. In this sermon Wesley lays out three central tenets on the correct way to interact with money: first, to earn all one can; second, to save all one can; and, third, to give all one can. Wesley himself lived this out in his own life, earning a fortune many times and continually giving it away. At the end of his life he owned one coat and two silver spoons (Templeton, 2011:6).

Earning all one can was not about acquisitiveness for Wesley, but about participating in the world (and therefore in God's work). It was important to earn wealth in ways that did not cause suffering to oneself, to others or indeed to the 'creation' (the world). Wesley said: 'We ought to gain all we can ... But this it is certain we ought not to do; we ought not to gain money at the expense of life, nor (which is in effect the same thing) at the expense of our health. Therefore, no gain whatsoever should induce us to enter into, or to continue in, any employ, which is of such a kind, or is attended with so hard or so long labour, as to impair our constitution.' In his definition of 'health' he included not only the physical body, but also 'the spirit of an healthful mind'. In a similar vein he speaks of not hurting our neighbour in his body or his soul – 'We cannot, if we love everyone as ourselves, hurt anyone *in his substance*' (1961:16).

Saving all one can was not about hoarding or investing – Wesley was certainly not suggesting the sin of the miser need not be considered a sin – but rather about a simplified lifestyle, without extravagance or self-gratification (which is why Templeton's particular interpretation of Wesley's use of the Parable of the Talents does not quite ring true). According to Wesley, anything one had that was unnecessary had been gained 'through the blood of the poor', so forgoing hoarding was a way of giving to the poor. Wesley was not without politics of course, and fought to 'give voice to the voiceless'. Hence the appeal of Methodism to the poor, the dispossessed and the newly self-aware working class. It is clear to see how such a message held appeal for the working classes; it is not dissimilar in fact to Karl Marx writing about wealthy capitalists in terms of 'vampires' sucking the blood of the workers![12] Financial prudence became a political stance on the painful labour of the working man. Wesley said, 'Save all you can. Do not throw the precious talent into the sea: Leave that folly to heathen philosophers. Do not throw it away in idle expenses, which is just the same as throwing it into the sea. Expend no part of it merely to gratify the desire of the flesh, the desire of the eye, or the pride of life' (1961:21).

Finally, giving all one can was about seeing love as an emptying out of oneself on behalf of others; one cannot love without giving. Wesley acknowledged that charity could be paternalistic, but insisted that giving was about justice, broadly conceived of as equality, or as Wesley put it, ensuring that everyone had a place at the table of God and could partake of God's provisions. In addition, of course, giving, unlike charity, was about stewardship and seeing one's body and life as a vessel of God's. Wesley said, 'Then give all you can. In order to see the ground and reason of this, consider, when the Possessor of heaven and earth brought you into being, and placed you in this world, he placed you here not as a proprietor, but a steward: As such he entrusted you, for a season, with goods of various kinds; but the sole property of these still rests in him, nor can be alienated from him. As you yourself are not your own, but his, such is, likewise, all that you enjoy. Such is your soul and your body, not your own, but God's' (1961:23).

This idea of being a steward, not an owner, of material objects (and indeed of one's own body!) is key to the Methodist version of thrift. Wesley's emphasis on giving for justice was a powerful counter to capitalism, and in many ways to the idea of oneself as a potent and empowered individual. However, essentially in his first tenet ('make all you can') he was legitimising capitalism, rather than strategically using it. His conception was that the way to engage with life most fully was to make all you can – a fundamentally pro-capitalist stance. Yet he recognised that 'gaining all one can' could lead to greed and boredom and thus away from the path to heaven. It was for this reason that 'giving all one could' was also so important, this meant the more one gained, the more one gave, the better one felt, the more useful one was to society, and the greater the treasure awaiting one in heaven. Indeed, towards his death, when Methodism had over 50,000 followers in England and was rapidly growing in America, Wesley became worried that it would exist only in name after his death. Specifically, he was concerned that this would be due to the increasing wealth of Methodists. He witnessed the way in which Methodism made people diligent and frugal, and that with this wealth increased. This presented a serious threat, not only to Methodism, but to Christianity more generally in his view. He was concerned that his third point in 'The Uses of Money' – give away all you can – was being ignored. In 'Thoughts upon Methodism', in 1786, he wrote, 'Methodists in every place grow diligent and frugal; consequently they increase in goods. Hence, they proportionately increase in pride, in anger, in the desire of the flesh, the desire of the eyes, and the pride of life. So, although the form of religion remains, the spirit is swiftly vanishing away' (1786).

Probably, Wesley had reason to worry. Methodism did not hold the seeds of genuine change in socio-economic structures that it did in many others (such as its immediate and strong stance against slavery). The issue was, arguably, inherent in Wesley's own attitudes towards, and preaching on, money. He was, essentially, a very successful capitalist who, despite a strong sympathy for the working person, did not see it as an implicitly unjust and corrupt system, but rather as a tool for living. (In this he was not dissimilar to Benjamin Franklin, of whom he was almost a direct contemporary, being born three years before him, and dying one year after him.) Returning to the Parable of the Talents, one might ask, what was so wrong with the behaviour of the third talent? Why not simply gain less and enjoy the additional time one might have on one's hands? That, too, could see one use one's days wisely and to the benefit of others, and would most certainly guard against greed. Perhaps the third talent had more agency even, due to not attempting to be part of an economic system whose negative aspect then needed compensating for by giving away to others what we have earnt.

Religion and individualism

It is tempting to leave this chapter with the impression that the religious notions of thrift explored here were (and often still are) essentially about belief systems that rebuked unfettered profit, and the chasing of profit that harmed others. Self-denial was certainly a part of Puritan, Quaker and Methodist thrift, but there are important distinctions to be made here when analysing these aspects in light of present-day thinking on thrift. As chapter 7 will show, Wesley's key message of earning all you can, saving all you can and spending all you can has become embroiled in various American religious denominations' teachings and is often quoted by those in the Voluntary Simplicity movement. Much Quaker activism is concerned with ethical consumption and more egalitarian ways of doing business. Meanwhile, many contemporary commentators link Puritanism to the ideas behind today's consumer-capitalism, especially that of the United States. Thrift today, in these three conceptions then, is driven by very different desires – for charity, social reform and the holy trilogy of capitalism, democracy and the free market.

The former two leanings require less explanation and will be picked up on in other chapters. The Puritan legacy is more crucial for an analysis of thrift as frugality in the West today. Indeed, for contemporary commentator Jim Sleeper, the Puritans have never been more relevant. He argues that they acutely anticipated present dilemmas and strengths in America, and that 'Puritan premises and practices gestated and channeled some of the liberal-capitalist premises, practices, and paradoxes that are now embraced and reviled the world over' (2015:57). Similarly, Mark Noll asserts that the republican conviction of belief in the reciprocity of personal morality and social well-being was essentially a Puritan trait. Whilst he acknowledges that changes in what was considered personal morality took place over time, what underlay those changes was 'a remarkably fixed alliance between a language of liberty and a language of virtue' (Noll, 2001). Sleeper links these twin paradigms of liberty and virtue to Alexis de Tocqueville, saying 'as Puritans thus struggled to ground their salvation-hungry faith in covenanted, earthbound communities of law and work, they catalyzed the broader, distinctively American conviction that individual liberty and religious commitment reinforce and even need each other, instead of opposing each other' (Tocqueville, 2003:58). Tocqueville famously explained the conjunction of religion and wealth as the result of two distinct elements that had, in other countries, been seen to contradict each other, but which in America had been successfully combined – the spirit of religion and the spirit of liberty (2003). Here, Tocqueville is of course placing the quest for wealth as part of that for liberty, a line of thinking that continued to far more contemporary proponents such as Milton Friedman, and which can be seen as existing throughout the West as a result.

The seeds of this alliance may well have started to be sewn in the 1920s – the decade of relative plenty sandwiched between the First World War and the Great Depression. In 1925, advertising man Bruce Barton wrote *The Man Nobody Knows*. Essentially, the book cast Jesus Christ as the best possible example for American business, equating his parables with advertising, his apostles as a sales force and Jesus himself as a world-class salesman. Barton argued, 'Jesus would be a national advertiser today. I am sure, as he was the great advertiser of his own day' (Barton, 1926: 140). Somewhat incredibly, the book was endorsed by notable clergy of the day. Barton has successfully enabled Americans to reconcile their religious beliefs with their attitudes towards commercial success. He had brought to life, and personified in Jesus, the Protestant ethic that Weber had first detailed. The book was a best-seller, selling over 500,000 copies. Similar-minded clergy were perhaps those enlisted in the 1930s by businessmen determined to fight Roosevelt's New Deal policies. As Kevin Kruze argues, such businessmen were encouraged to attack the New Deal as a perversion of the central principle of Christianity – the sanctity and salvation of the *individual*. For Kruze, this was part of an invention of Christian America that was sealed when Congress added the phrase 'under God' to the Pledge of Allegiance, and made 'In God We Trust' the country's first official motto (Kruze, 2016).

Individualism was the quality that emerged from the alliance between religion and liberty, and the quality that proves most problematic for conservative advocates of thrift (frugality) today, and indeed for those advocating an alternative to mainstream consumer capitalism. Puritanism played no small part in this. As Sleeper argues, 'Puritanism set up a creative tension between personal autonomy and communal obligation, impassioned conscience and sober humility, and vigorous enterprise and collective obligation' (2015:58). Or, as Tawney puts it, 'there was in Puritanism … a collectivism which grasped at an iron discipline, and an individualism which spurned the savorless mess of human ordinances' (2015). Indeed, the individualism proposed by Friedman was to begin its assent with the post-Puritan thinking of Benjamin Franklin. A direct contemporary of John Wesley, Franklin essentially secularised thrift, making it accessible even to those without religious inclination. Others of his era, in other parts of the West, would also play their parts in the individualisation of thrift, as the next chapter explores.

It is worth mentioning that in recent years there has been a small, but notable, stream of media coverage and publicity that opposes this mainstream thrust, and that is the narrative that posits Christianity as in some sense socialist, or at least concerned with a more equal distribution of wealth and a concern for those less well off. (This is not to say that beneath this media coverage there is not of course a huge history of Christianity as socialist, or indeed millions of individuals who perceive this to be the case.) Recently, there has been renewed interest in St Paul as a figure who had much to say about money, and who appears to have challenged the early Christian church in some ways, not least by refusing to take payment for his preaching.[13] A significant body of literature has emerged, not only around Paul's thought, but also around the significance of Paul's fundraising venture for the poor in Jerusalem – 'the collection'. (See, for example, Verlyn Verbrugge and Keith Krell's 2015 book – *Paul and Money* – which presents an in-depth account of Paul's writings.) Much of this renewed interest followed the financial crisis of 2008, which spawned titles such as Ben Witherington's *Jesus and Money* – in which both faith-promise and health-and-wealth approaches are criticised in favour of a stewardship of possessions (impossible to read without hearing Wesleyan undertones to some extent) (Witherington, 2012).

Yet, despite these interesting new forays, the religious worldviews most clearly associated with thrift, and which have most clearly influenced ideas around the practice of thrift today, tend to seek individual change, or new ways of living within or on the edges of mainstream capitalist society in the 'developed world'. They appear to be consistently fighting against the threat of 'individualism' that will lead to an unfettered capitalism, but are themselves often inherently individualist at their core. Indeed, it is difficult to find an interpretation of Christianity that does not essentially suggest that the rich are responsible for the poor and should give to them. Whilst this may be redistributive it is not revolutionary; no texts suggest changing a system that creates rich and poor in the first place.

The problem perhaps is that in so many of the religious denominations that have emphasised thrift, there is an idea that at some level wealth *ought* to be gained. This is not to say it should not, or to advocate a religious poverty mentality – such binaries are too simplistic. Rather, the concern here is that if fundamentally a religious message says one *ought to* (and indeed *can*) attempt to create wealth for oneself, then there is a pervasive idea, consistently resurfacing, that everyone can practise thrift; that one simply needs to work out where all the money goes and then reign it in. There is no acknowledgement that many people simply genuinely do not have enough money to make ends meet after they have paid for the absolute essentials in their lives. As Oscar Wilde said, 'Sometimes the poor are praised for being thrifty. But to recommend thrift to the poor is both grotesque and insulting. It is like advising a man who is starving to eat less' (2001). It is almost impossible, even once we travel far from the Puritans and Methodists into lifestyle thrifters, to get away from this moral righteousness. In fact, with the exception of some current-day politically radical Quakers, few of these positions fully represent an attempt to return to a thrift based on thriving, largely because few of them seek genuine social change, preferring instead to use their own excess to temper or reform an existing unjust system.

3

Individualist thrift: Benjamin Franklin, Samuel Smiles and Victorian moralism

Benjamin Franklin and the secularisation of thrift

The onset of a more individualistic rationale for thrift can in large part be attributed to a secularisation of the concept. The direct aim of Puritan thrift was not to make profit, but to do what was moral and right under the eyes of God. However, as the Augustinian sense of Puritan thought began to win through, making profit became increasingly acceptable as a way to guard against other 'evils' – even in the eyes of the Puritans. Besides, as the nineteenth century progressed, this specifically religious motivation for thrift became more aligned to a general sense of social morality typified by Victorian middle-class attitudes. As Yates and Hunter put it, Puritan thrift gave way to 'classic thrift' – an emphasis on the morality of the individual's financial behaviour (2011). They argue that it was at this moment that 'thrift and this [pan-Protestant] ethical sensibility gradually detached themselves from the Puritan providentialist cosmology that originally underwrote them. Thrift in this dispensation found new sanction in a rich and dynamic amalgamation of civic republican, Protestant, Stoic, and democratic sensibilities, but it did so primarily as a private affair' (2011:13). Liberated from providentialism, and the sense that one's place in heaven (or not) was determined from birth, the practice of thrift, if in any sense religious, became a way to *secure* a place in heaven one had not yet been given, as opposed to merely keeping the place one already had. In the nineteenth century one *worked* (and thrifted) one's way into heaven. However, on the whole, classic thrift was not only less directly religious, but despite being about what was right for society, was almost exclusively concerned with the behaviour of individuals. Individual responsibility, under this new conception of thrift, rather than guaranteeing one's place in heaven, was what determined the success or failure of a whole society and economy.

The great inventor of post-Puritan thrift was Benjamin Franklin – author, printer, political theorist, inventor, politician and, of course, president of

Pennsylvania and one of the founding fathers of the United States.[1] He stood as thrift's greatest exponent for at least two centuries – 'he personified it, practiced it, promoted it, and, through his translated writings,[2] exported it to the rest of the world' where it was keenly received and became a staple in school classrooms (Blankenhorn et al., 2009:10). Franklin was born in 1706 in Boston, Massachusetts, to strict Puritan parents – Josiah and Abiah. His father owned a copy of the book by famous Puritan founding father Cotton Mather, entitled *Bonifacius: Essays to do Good*, and this was to prove a huge influence on Franklin, largely by convincing him of the importance of forming do-good associations in order to benefit society (Isaacson, 2003:26). He was also greatly influenced by the Puritan belief that all men are created equals, and all can be saved. He embraced the first part of this as part of a radical (for the time) notion of egalitarian democracy, but rejected the salvation element. In fact, when Franklin formulated his beliefs in 1728, the publication did not mention many of the traditional Puritan beliefs, such as that of the belief in salvation, the divinity of Jesus and religious dogma.[3] Indeed, his autobiography of 1771 stated that he saw himself as a deist, i.e. rejecting revelation as a form of religious knowledge, and believing instead in the power of reason and observation of the natural world to prove the existence of a single Creator (Franklin, 2012b). As a result, Franklin's thrift is essentially secular in its logic and morals.

If Franklin's thinking was rather challenging when considered in the light of his strict Puritan upbringing, his actions were perhaps even more rebellious. At the age of twenty-four he set up a common-law marriage to Deborah Read, taking in his illegitimate son from another relationship, as well as fathering two more children with Deborah. He also became involved in radical politics during his time in London between the mid-1750s and the mid-1770s, as a member of 'the honest Whigs' group (Isaacson, 2003). Yet his '13 virtues' that he attempted to live by (often, by his own admission, failing), were broadly in line with the more cultural concerns of Puritanism. They were: temperance, silence, order, resolution, frugality, industry, sincerity, justice, moderation, cleanliness, tranquillity, chastity and humility. Thrift then, was clearly established as frugality by Franklin, but perhaps more poignantly, was grouped with industry and moderation, making it part of a cycle in which hard work brought a living that should be used extremely carefully and without any decadence. Franklin's famous Poor Richard maxims prove this brilliantly. Poor Richard (or Richard Saunders) was a character created by Benjamin Franklin, and who appeared in his best-selling almanac that ran from 1732 to 1758.[4] The almanac contained a calendar, weather, poems, sayings and astrological information typical of almanacs of the period, but also featured Franklin's aphorisms and proverbs, many of them about industry and frugality.

On industry and leisure Poor Richard espouses: 'Employ thy time well, if thou meanest to gain leisure; and, since thou art not sure of a minute, throw not away an hour'; 'Do not squander time, for that is the stuff life is made of'; 'The sleeping fox catches no poultry'; and 'there will be sleeping enough in the grave'. He even suggests that industry prolongs life: 'Idleness taxes many of us much more; sloth, by bringing on diseases, absolutely shortens life' and 'Early to bed, and early to rise, makes a man healthy, wealthy, and wise'. On moderation and frugality: 'Many a little makes a mickle'; 'A small leak will sink a great ship'; and 'Buy what thou hast no need of, and ere long thou shalt sell thy necessaries'. And perhaps most tellingly in terms of the way in which thrift as frugality is posited as an individual enterprise, with the individual taking the first action, and God's action following: 'God helps them that help themselves.' Indeed Franklin/Poor Richard did not espouse any notion that individual behaviour may have an effect on society as a whole, even though this may well have been Franklin's motivation considering the times of national debt in which he lived.[5]

This was, then, a thrift that pervaded many elements of everyday life; a thrift that was about never being 'showy' or indulging in laziness (or perhaps even relaxation!). But what made this thrift *post*-Puritan was Franklin's lack of belief in salvation, specifically his rejection of the Calvinist teaching that we are all destined to go to heaven *unless* we do something wrong. For Franklin, salvation was earned, from scratch, through our own efforts, and as individuals; it was no longer the case that we were all going to heaven together unless we fell short of the criteria through our own doing. As Blankenhorn *et al.* assert, 'Franklin's thrift became the cornerstone of a new kind of secular faith in the individual's capacity to shape his or her own lot and fortune in life' (2009:4). So, whereas for Franklin's Calvinist forebears, God had the power to deny already-granted access, for Franklin, the distribution of material blessings would no longer 'be subject to the mysterious workings of God's grace nor to the mere accidents of fortunate birth. The way to wealth rested in the cultivation of habits of industry and frugality' (Blankenhorn *et al.*, 2009:4). So, it was with Franklin's post-Puritanism that thrift became clearly established as not only linked to industry and moderation, but also to frugality. Furthermore, this frugality was construed as essentially the responsibility of the individual or the household. Indeed, Franklin tended to see thrift as a wifely duty, envisioning the household as the primary unit of society and marriage as an economic partnership in which it was the duty of the wife, as the person mainly concerned with the household, to promote industry and frugality (Franklin, 1728). In this way, thrift began to be related to the *organisation* of everyday life and the seeds were sown for the judging of individuals and households as economically and therefore morally irresponsible. For Franklin, however, this is not *explicitly* a societal problem (although he may well have recognised it as such and decided not to include that in his writings), rather, it is simply foolish on the part of the individual involved who only has him or herself to blame for future poverty.

This sense of individual or family responsibility means Franklin's Poor Richard maxims are seen by many as foundational for the American dream (see Blankenhorn *et al.*, 2009:5–6), and the sense of individual striving or 'self-help' contained within them is no small part of that. Blankenhorn *et al.* praise Franklin for the way in which he both reflected the American mentality and shaped it into what we now call the 'American Dream', arguing that he 'revealed dispositions that reflected not just his own character but the American character itself: the passion for freedom, the aspiration for self-improvement, the pragmatic approach to problems, the desire to do good, and the confident outlook on the future' (Blankenhorn *et al.*, 2009:5). They reject the claim that Franklin promoted an outmoded, crabbed and narrowly economistic vision of human purpose and possibility, arguing instead that Franklin's thinking on industry and frugality provided a 'social philosophy of human flourishing and freedom rooted in social mobility, economic opportunity, and generosity to others' (2009:5). This gathers some credence when we consider that in his later life Franklin himself was by no means frugal, arguing that he had saved for half his life in order that he might have the freedom to spend in the other half. In fact, freedom was a key element for Franklin's thrift – industry and frugality were not ends in themselves, but rather, part of a road to economic freedom and, crucially, free time. However, this is hardly the 'human flourishing' (eudaimonia) first encountered in Aristotle, whose notion was rooted in concerns with the ability to develop one's highest or most human capabilities.[6] This grand aspiration hardly compares to Franklin's rather everyday pragmatism. That said, there are similarities between the two; for example, for Aristotle, human flourishing must involve activity in accordance with Reason – the most obvious example of this, he says, being work.[7]

Others do not so readily buy this idea of Franklin as the calculated hedonist, and are not so complimentary towards him. Mark Twain wrote that Franklin inflicted suffering on generations of boys who had to live by his maxims (1870); D. H. Lawrence called Franklin a 'snuff-coloured little man' who took the unruly passions of humankind and forced them into a narrow moral accounting system of credits and debits (1933). Max Weber attacked Franklin for preaching a gospel of money as an end in itself and therefore promoting a secular philosophy of avarice and crude utilitarianism. He argues, 'The peculiarity of this philosophy of avarice [witnessed in Franklin's writings on thrift] appears to be the ideal of the honest man of recognized credit, and above all the idea of the duty of the individual toward the increase of his capital, which is assumed as an end in itself' (1992:91). It is certainly tempting to simply see Franklin as a hypocrite, no more excusable than any of the other proponents of thrift we will meet in this book, but simply more likeable (for some!) not least because his ideas about economic independence remain so central to American identity. As Blankenhorn *et al.* say, 'if Jefferson wrote the Declaration of Independence and Madison crafted the Constitution, then Benjamin Franklin, it might truly be said, invented the American Dream' (2009:5–6).

At first glance, the most radical element in Franklin's version of thrift is the idea that the passing of wealth and privilege onto future generations is to blame for creating such wide divisions between rich and poor. This aspect Franklin found vicious and demoralising for both, writing in the words of Poor Richard 'the poor have little, beggars none, the rich too much, enough not one'. Both, according to Franklin, lived only for the pleasures of the moment, and it was therefore the 'middling ranks' that offered most hope for society. Franklin emphasised the ability of the middle classes to show the 'others' how they should live, yet believed that, in an ideal world, this would lead to a narrower gap between rich and poor as the short-termism and profligacy of both the rich and the poor (in their different ways) enabled them to live out the notion so dear to him that all men are born equal. As will be seen later in this chapter, there is much in this that is similar to Samuel Smiles' thinking. Smiles too felt the middle classes were those to be emulated, and that all men were equal; he too hoped to lessen the gap between rich and poor through the poor helping themselves.

However, as with Smiles, there was a moral superiority and judgemental attitude at the forefront of all Franklin's thinking that failed to acknowledge the intractable situations some of those living in poverty faced. Essentially, Franklin, like Smiles, believed that anyone, regardless of how harsh or basic their situation was, could work their way out of poverty. Furthermore, this failure was based in a worldview that paid little attention to the structural factors that caused these situations of poverty to be so intractable. For Franklin, the individual held immense agency, and whilst he spoke of the culture of debt in America at the time, he saw it as entirely possible to resist through hard work and individual effort. He clung to his belief in the possibility of all men to be 'self-made' with a tenacity that saw other contributing factors melt away. Matthew Garrett, for example, reminds us of how the lack of presence of Franklin's (well-off and socially prominent) mother in his autobiography speaks of 'the chasm between Franklinian success and the social cost of the competition on which it is based' (2013:519).

Dickens, Wharton and other social critics of the 'gilded age'

Franklin's influence in the area of economic responsibility spread far and can be witnessed not least in the literature of the era and those that directly followed, that capture this new moralistic individualism perfectly. Vernon Parrington argues that Daniel Defoe's Robinson Crusoe, a 'practical efficient man making himself master of his environment' was the dream of Defoe to Franklin's 'visible, new-world embodiment of that dream' (1927:166). In addition, Parrington sees Defoe's *Essay on Projects* as a classic document of the rising middle class, arguing 'it might well have been Franklin's first textbook' (1927:166). In the essay Defoe advocates a plan for the formation of mutual assistance societies, and so pre-empted or perhaps even inspired the formation of life insurance companies and Friendly Societies.

In Britain Susannah Carter published *The Frugal Housewife* in 1765, whilst in America Lydia Child wrote *The Frugal Housewife: Dedicated to Those Who Are Not Ashamed of Economy* in 1829 (changed to *The American Frugal Housewife* in 1832 to end the confusion with the British author). Child's book was expanded and went through thirty-three printings in twenty-five years – a testament to the popularity of the thrift discourse throughout this era. In a similar vein, Catherine Beecher wrote *A Treatise on Domestic Economy* in 1842 and co-authored *The American Woman's Home* with her sister Harriet in 1869.[8] In addition, Isabella Beeton ('Mrs Beeton') published her famous 'cookbook' in 1861, although as Christopher Clausen points out, it was initially far more than a cookbook, as it was entitled *Mrs Beeton's book of household management* and expounded on the proper roles for a cook, valet, kitchenmaid, footman and more (Clausen, 1993). In it, she marks out frugality and economy as home virtues, coining the phrase, 'a place for everything and everything in its place' (see 1993:412).

Such publications spoke to that quintessential desire of the Victorian age – respectability – and concerned themselves with a realm of everyday objects and activities that might perhaps usefully be categorised neither as necessities, nor as 'niceties', but rather as what Smith called 'decencies' in that they provided a certain level of respectability (2003). They also solidly linked thrift to household economia, and to the role of the woman. A 'good woman' was one who was capable of frugality, as Franklin himself had believed. Indeed, this was a version of womanhood that was to prove incredibly pervasive, arguably making its way into current-day rhetoric on household thrift under austerity, as this book will show.

Charles Dickens too promoted thrift, presenting characters that came undone due to either their miserly, or their reckless, financial behaviour. Scrooge, of course, in *A Christmas Carol*, was typical of the former, as was the recognition of William Dorrit in *Little Dorrit* when he said 'I am the only child of parents who weighed, measured, and priced everything; for whom what could not be weighed, measured, and priced, had no existence' (Dickens, 1996:47). Pip and the debt he gets into in *Great Expectations* provides a good example of the latter, and Dickens' attitudes are well-reflected in his description of Ralph Nickleby in *Nicholas Nickleby* as a man for whom 'gold conjures up a mist … more destructive of all his old senses and lulling to his feelings than the fumes of charcoal' (Dickens, 2013:3). Perhaps most indicative of Dickens' attitude towards thrift though are the words of Mr Micawber in *David Copperfield*: 'Annual income twenty pounds, annual expenditure nineteen [pounds] nineteen [shillings] and six [pence], result happiness. Annual income twenty pounds, annual expenditure twenty pounds ought and six, result misery' (Dickens, 1992:153).[9]

In Edith Wharton's novels in the twentieth century we are presented with visions of a domestic asceticism which serve to counter-balance, and critique, the decadence of the wealthy. As Carol Singley, a well-known Wharton scholar, argues, the rise of the thrift movement at the end of the nineteenth century and its expansion through the first decades of the twentieth century 'coincide with Wharton's vast production of novels, short stories, essays, and books of nonfiction, in which she … exposes the distorted social and economic priorities of an increasingly commodified culture' (2019).[10] For Singley, Wharton's work embodies the principles of both Franklin and Smiles in its adherence to a notion of thrift as economy that can secure independence, as being associated solely with miserliness. She argues that Wharton's most successful characters always embrace this ethos, whilst her least successful ones ignore it at their peril. This is most clearly witnessed in Wharton's novel *The House of Mirth*, in which Lily Bart, a beautiful young society woman, seeks a wealthy husband in order to save her family from financial ruin. Lily travels from one social setting to another, but fails to capitalise on various opportunities to marry, and spirals downwards in social and economic value until she dies alone of a drug overdose in a boarding house.

Children's books of a slightly later period were also very keen to promote thrift. Laura Roundtree-Smith wrote *Nan and Ann in Thrift Town* (1925). Meanwhile, Joseph Sindelar published *Father Thrift and his Animal Friends* (1918). There were even board games teaching thrift. Nineteenth-century creation 'The Mansion of Happiness' (1843) was based on Puritan principles and had squares one landed on labelled, for example, 'the road to folly' if you spent too much (Hoffer, 2003). This can be interesting when compared to the later 'Game of Life' (1860) in which players were rewarded for attending college, being elected to Congress and getting rich. Secular virtues such as thrift, ambition and neatness received more emphasis than religious virtues (Hoffer, 2003). In the present day, Hasbro's 'Game of Life' sees players given a credit card which enables them to play whilst hugely in debt, and indeed potentially even win despite that fact.

Samuel Smiles and economic morality

Of all the literature of the era, however, the most influential (certainly in Britain) was that of Samuel Smiles. His first book – *Self-Help* (1859) – was a bestseller that had, almost overnight, elevated him to celebrity status. His second – *Thrift* (1875) – was in many ways a continuation of his first, and although not quite as popular, placed an emphasis on good self-management and personal propriety that was irresistible to a Victorian readership keen to capitalise upon a highly moralistic worldview. A raft of bestsellers followed; books that tapped with alacrity into the spirit of the times.[11] Smiles' polemic was perfect for the audience of the era, coming as it did from a man who is often characterised as a classic Victorian; an outcome of what Jackson Lears calls the 'Victorian-Individualist Synthesis' (1995). By this Lears means the specific historical mix of economic growth and consumerism, the rise of the middle class, and anxiety over consumerism and luxury on civic values. Such social changes were to lead to an emphasis on self-discipline, hard work, sobriety, honesty, diligence and industry, as well as a morally inflected striving for respectability. (Many social housing movements of the time saw those classified as 'semi-criminal' striving to get into housing estates for the respectable poor, not simply to gain better housing, but also to achieve the respectability that was so important at the time.) Yet Smiles is a far more complicated character than Lears might like to imagine. His life is often described as divided into a far more radical earlier period, and a pragmatic later period, yet as what follows will explore, many commentators now interpret his work as a far more nuanced political stance that reflected a personal struggle between the desire for societal change and the advocacy of individual reform.

Born in 1812, one of eleven siblings in East Lothian, Smiles was given a strongly Cameronian upbringing that instilled in him the importance of proper behaviour.[12] His father had died in the cholera epidemic of 1832 and Smiles therefore witnessed his mother work ceaselessly in a general store – an income that would support the studies of his young adulthood. He began his career as an author in 1837 by writing articles for the *Edinburgh Weekly Chronicle* and the *Leeds Times* in which he campaigned for parliamentary reform. This was to become a major feature of his life and, in May 1840, he became secretary to the Leeds Parliamentary Reform Association, an organisation that held to the six objectives of Chartism: universal suffrage for all men over the age of twenty-one; equal-sized electoral districts; voting by secret ballot; an end to the need of MPs to qualify for parliament, other than by winning an election; pay for MPs; and annual parliaments. He became editor of the *Leeds Times* in 1838, where he advocated radical causes ranging from women's suffrage to free trade.

By the late 1840s, however, Smiles became concerned about the avocation of physical force by Chartists Feargus O'Connor and George Julian Harney, although he seems to have agreed with them that the movement's current tactics were not effective. He married in 1843, and in 1845 left the *Leeds Times* to become a secretary for Leeds and Thirsk Railway (Mackay, 1905).[13] By the 1850s he seems to have completely given up on parliamentary reform and other structural changes as a means of social advance. He was frustrated with the powerful institutions of his time, and was, it seems, a man struggling with his own, and others', inability to create societal change. For the rest of his career, he advocated *individual* responsibility and self-improvement, not so much because he thought this the proper course, but because he perhaps saw it as the *only* course (Jarvis, 1997). It was, perhaps, indicative of a deep disappointment with his own attempts to change society, as much as what he saw as a highly positive harnessing of the individual's motivations in life.

This switch in emphasis from the public to the private realm, and indeed therefore from government politics to the conduct of individuals, was to prove key in forming the basic tenets of his books *Self-Help* (1859) and *Thrift* (1875). However, many argue that the public and private were more organically linked in Smiles' thought and the times he lived in than early commentators on his work tended to argue. For example, whilst he acknowledges that there did develop in Smiles' thought two different *avenues* to reform, Tim Travers argues most convincingly that Smiles' work does not in fact present a dilemma between personal reform and moral values on one hand, and societal political and legislative change on the other (Travers, 1977:164). He asserts that in contrast to the popular view of Smiles as a 'convenient example of mid-Victorian individualism and middle-class values', his work, especially *Self-Help*, shows how Smiles, and others at the time, felt that political and personal reform were not mutually exclusive (1977:161). For Travers, this same reconciliation between personal moral reform and political reform can be seen in the lives of Chartists such as Lowery, Vincent, O'Neill and Lovett (1977:164). For Travers the explanation for this is to be found in the combination of Smiles' early Scottish background and Calvinist training, with its emphasis on personal reform and moral values, and the influence of Enlightenment concepts stimulated by the events surrounding the reform act of 1832 and pushing for legislative change (1977:161–164). The presence of Enlightenment thinking in the Victorian age is similarly argued by Trygve Tholfsen, in 'The Intellectual Origins of Mid-Victorian Stability' (1971); whilst Franklin Baumer uses the term 'the New Enlightenment' to describe the new liberals and reformers of the nineteenth century, including John Stuart Mill, the Philosophic Radicals and Samuel Smiles.

R. J. Morris explains Smiles' position as one informed by his own membership of the nineteenth-century petit bourgeoisie, who 'at some time around 1850, abandoned radicalism and lost their initiative in politics', often becoming absorbed in Gladstone's Liberal Party (1981:89). For Smiles, this was not least due to the failure of projects such as the Leeds Redemption Society which he supported, and which had created a short-lived community on a hillside in south Wales. The society was influenced by experimental and utopian radicals such as John Mills, and had planned to purchase land near Leeds and build factories, workshops and freehold housing for their members, as well as provide education and a burial at the end of each member's life (Morris, 1981:105–106). However, lack of capital and an unsuitable site meant the society failed to develop and Smiles had to face the reality that a small society working against dominant social structures seemed doomed to be defeated by administrative and financial problems. In the beginning paragraphs of *Self-Help* he argues that 'even the best institutions can give man no active help', and that 'the function of government is negative and restrictive, rather than positive and active' (2012:8).

Morris concludes therefore that the concept of self-help was not an expression of mid-Victorian confidence and optimism, but rather 'a form of lower middle-class utopianism, which sublimated the frustrated political ambition of the petit bourgeois radicals of the 1840s', following the failures of cooperative projects such as those mentioned above (1981:90–91). It was, he says, a 'charter by which the lower middle classes and prosperous working classes might restore their self-respect after the defeats of the 1840s' (1981:108–109). Furthermore, it was the only way in which this group could escape the authority of the ruling class and the mass violence and degrading poverty of the lower classes – it really did seem that only their own efforts would achieve results for them. For Morris, the popularity of *Self-Help* suggests that 'many men emerged from the 1840s with the same moral needs and narrow but active social vision which had been created by Smiles' experiences in Leeds' (1981:108–109). Adrian Jarvis, however, challenges this view, arguing that Smiles never claimed the remedy for the nation lay *solely* in the reform of a corrupt and incompetent government, nor did he claim later in life that it lay *solely* in the hands of the individual (1997:39).

Either way, it is clear that Smiles' later emphasis on individualism was not a straightforwardly Victorian moralistic stance. Certainly, Smiles linked the self-made man to the idea of perseverance – an idea that had come to him when he wrote the biography of engineer George Stephenson, who he frequently quoted as persuading others to persevere and who could not, Smiles felt, have achieved his great engineering feat without that quality (Smiles, 1857). And, as Trendafilov argues, perseverance was a concept which almost undoubtedly appealed to him due to his religious Calvinist family upbringing, being an old theological term that stems from the doctrine of the 'perseverance of the saints' as it was first outlined by St Augustine, in *On the Gift of Perseverance*, and was later elaborated on by Calvin, among others (2015:5).[14] However, Smiles' version of perseverance as witnessed in both *Self-Help* and *Thrift* was more deeply inspired by a far less likely (for Smiles) source – the thinking of transcendentalists such as Ralph Waldo Emerson and William Channing.[15]

Alexander Tyrrell's (1970) account provides the best testament to this influence on Smiles. In 'The Origins of a Bestseller: An Unacknowledged Debt', he provides evidence that in 1839, three months after he had become editor of the *Leeds Times*, Smiles published a highly positive review of Channing's recent publication *Self-Culture* (see Smiles, 'The Education of the People', 1839). Morris argues that for Smiles, the concept of self-culture fulfilled the 'moral, religious, intellectual and social nature of man, and could be achieved by the control of animal appetites, by overcoming hardship and by the fellowship of good books' (1981:95). In fact, despite being criticised for a lack of practicality, self-culture held great appeal for Smiles because it 'made a virtue of ignoring material difficulties and social pressures' (1981:94–95). Morris also makes the case that these writings were appealing to Smiles and other 'radicals' because they enabled them 'to acknowledge such religious feelings as had survived the rejection of priestcraft, and still come to terms with industrial society as they saw it' (1981:94–95).

In addition, Tyrrell points to the use of the term self-help in Emerson's *Man the Reformer* – a public address Emerson delivered to a Boston mechanics' institute and published a year later. In this address, Emerson asks, 'Can not we learn the lesson of self-help? Society is full of infirm people, whom incessantly summon others to serve them. They contrive everywhere to exhaust for their single comfort the entire means and appliances of the luxury to which our invention has yet attained … meantime, they never bestir themselves to serve another person, not they! They have a great deal more to do for themselves than they can possibly perform' (Emerson, 1841). It is not difficult to see how these words, more inspired by romantic individualism than they sound to our ears now, could have been interpreted by Smiles as a form of liberal emphasis on social climbing. Indeed, as Trendafilov asserts, 'the passage sounds like a restatement of the entire Smilesian doctrine as it is expounded in *Self-Help*: that governmental control mars the character of the individuals who comprise society, that living standard and success in life are personal objectives which can be achieved almost only on an individual basis' (2015:5). Indeed, Smiles' work inspired authors such as Orison Swett Marden, who were coming from a perspective that put far more emphasis on thriving and personal growth. Marden, for example, published many books, including *Thrift, Economy, and Cheerfulness as a Life Power* (1899), and was an early advocate of what would later become known as 'the power of positive thinking' (a term actually attributable to Norman Vincent Peale). In 'Be Good to Yourself', he writes rather poetically and sensitively about thrift, saying 'thrift is neither extravagance nor meanness. It is being good to ourselves in as large and scientific way as possible. Whatever cuts down power, whatever depletes our vitality, whatever cuts down our energy, is a niggardly, vicious economy or a wicked dissipation. Thrift means you should always have the best you can possibly afford, when the thing has any reference to your physical and mental health, to your growth in efficiency and power' (Marden, 1899).

Regardless of whether this was simply a bad interpretation of Emerson's point on the part of Smiles, it remains the case that transcendentalism inspired Smiles in a rather different way than it did Henry Thoreau, to say the least, as the chapter on spiritual thrift will make abundantly clear. In fact, it is quite incredible that such different historical characters should find a common point of departure and that it manifested through their writing in such different ways. For Smiles, the poor must work and save within capitalism; for Thoreau, they must attempt to leave the capitalistic system altogether. In fact, Smiles' conservative interpretation of Emerson forms an almost perfect trajectory to British ex-Prime Minister David Cameron's 'Big Society', in which small, local groups were envisaged as being empowered to take action and sort out their own local problems with their own initiative. In fact, despite acknowledgements as to the complicated and nuanced nature of Smiles' political position, there is little doubt that his work has been more successfully engineered to fit the purposes of the political Right than that of the political Left in the current day. A cursory glance over his key arguments quickly reveals how this was possible.

There is much that is appealing about Smiles' version of thrift. Primarily, thrift was about improving oneself (and not simply by social climbing) and gaining independence from one's employer. Smiles was genuinely against making money for its own sake, emphasising above all the importance and potential agency of saving for the future. Essentially, Smiles did not want people to be at the behest of the rich, or of charity, because he wanted them to have independence which would mean they were 'free'. In *Thrift*, he argued, 'Thrift is in no way connected to avarice, usury, greed or selfishness. It is, in fact, the very reverse of these disgusting dispositions. It means economy for the purpose of securing independence' (2007:56). So far so good. Unfortunately, this 'freedom' was to be achieved by essentially striving to be exactly like those who already had enough and, worse, trying to gain their approval by becoming 'respectable'! As Clausen argues, respectability for Smiles basically comes from 'turning away from the communal habits of the working classes' towards a home-centred and domestic life (1993:410). Not only does this seem to speak more loudly than all Smiles' more radical thoughts, reiterating rather finally the bourgeois individualism of thrift, but also it is also typical of how thrift in this era struggled again and again to remain a large, giving concept, instead continually being tied to notions of household economia and everyday accounting.

Clausen has few issues with this stance, seeing it as encapsulating 'a belief in the equal endowment of worth and talents among all social classes' and the availability of dignity for all who 'learn to seek it properly', further arguing that 'telling working class people that they merit the respect of others, should respect themselves, and can improve their lives through individual effort may be objectionable from the point of view of the revolutionary who wishes to abolish economic and social inequality at a stroke, but there is nothing inherently hypocritical or patronizing about it' (1993:406). However, regardless of whether one's politics are revolutionary or not, it is impossible not to maintain that Smiles' argument is certainly patronising if not slightly hypocritical in that he sees the attainment of respect as being achieved by the working classes adopting the habits and styles of the middle classes based on an acceptance that this is somehow inherently 'better'. Morris may argue that 'it is now rare for historians to represent this book [*Self-Help*] as a mere vulgar apologetic for middle-class wealth, power and neglect of the social welfare of the poor' (1981:90–91), but neither it is an entirely respectful and insightful portrayal of the working class.

He was of the firm belief by this stage of his life that poverty in many, if not most, instances was caused by habitual improvidence on the part of workers. Indeed, his attitude towards the working classes was thoroughly imbued with the belief that any poverty they experienced came as a result of their own lack of expediency. This dogmatic belief in the ability of all to save also impacted upon his attitude towards capitalists – a capitalist, according to Smiles, was simply someone 'who does not spend all that is earned by work' (2007:5). This rather excusing description of the capitalist likely came from his belief that thrift was not a natural instinct, and the admiration he therefore had for anyone who practised it. (Note how, true to his times, Smiles is caught up with what is 'natural' as opposed to the likely outcomes of material conditions.) As Donna Loftus argues, for Smiles, thrift 'encouraged independence, entrepreneurialism and the careful accounting of resources in the present for the future. He certainly mentioned nothing that provided even a nod to the Marxist conception of the capitalist as owning the means of production, or profiting from the labour of others. Thrift was then a way of promoting a more enduring capitalism, one that would build a stable society, foster a strong economy and promote national progress' (Loftus, 2019). In fact he directly relates the personal to the national, in doing so making the working class responsible for the nation's fate, saying 'national progress is the sum of individual industry, energy, and uprightness, as national decay is of individual idleness, selfishness, and vice' (Smiles, 2012:76). (Incidentally, as the concluding section of this chapter will show, this is a strangely similar rhetoric to that of David Cameron and George Osborne in their various speeches on austerity in the UK.)

The strong insinuation here is of course that all workers could become capitalists if they did but save some of their earnings; i.e. all salaries enable saving and anything not saved is necessarily 'frittered'. Smiles' concern was to make the working classes see that through prudential saving they could provide themselves with money to fall back on in hard times and therefore become more independent and less at the behest of their employers. His rhetoric, then, *appears* to be motivated by a desire for workers' freedom, as indeed did Franklin's before him, but is also enmeshed in the morals of the day that revolve around notions of laziness and deserving. This is shown through Smiles' contention that the working classes are capable of saving even on meagre incomes, but unable to achieve the independence this would bring them due in large part to their own irresponsible financial behaviour. So, whilst purportedly being concerned with the liberation of workers, Smiles' understanding of them was one that revolved around a largely patronising and judgemental attitude towards them. He argued, 'it will generally be found that men who are constantly lamenting their ill luck are only reaping the consequences of their own neglect, mismanagement, and improvidence, or want of application' (2007:35). In addition, despite a working-class start in life and a liberal-left sympathy for 'the poor man', underlying Smiles' advice on being thrifty in order to save for the future was a deeper and quite fundamental belief in the power of property-ownership to create reliable, responsible citizen-workers. Despite an ascetic feel to his prose then, he was essentially in agreement with the idea that encouraging consumption would make people less likely to fall into idleness. His faith in the moral righteousness of property ownership was only tempered by his desire for moderate wealth for the masses and his dislike of the rich.

The fact that in the twentieth century, Left-wing politicians harked back to Smiles work to extol the benefits of thrift in order to counter the Keynesian emphasis on consumerism and spending that began to prevail in the postwar years, whilst ignoring its obvious marketism in terms of property ownership and social climbing, only proves the extent to which there was a small-c conservativism and moralism to Labour Party rhetoric at the time. For example, in Britain, the Labour MP David Grenfell, in a debate on the Transitional Payments (Determination of Need) Bill, claimed that the 1932 bill 'discriminated not against the unthrifty, the idler, and the waster, but against the industrious, thrifty person, who had to pay a heavy penalty'. He accused the then Minister of Labour of penalising self-help and pouring contempt on the work of Samuel Smiles.

It is telling that the late Victorian and early twentieth century was the great era of thrift and savings organisations such as thrift societies and mutual savings banks. In America and Britain, charitable organisations promoting frugality became increasingly prevalent during the nineteenth century, largely as a response to the emphasis on individual responsibility. In 'Spreading the Gospel of Self-Denial: Thrift and Association in Antebellum America' (2011) Kathleen McCarthy charts the proliferation of charitable organisations in nineteenth-century America which promoted frugality in order to combat poverty. Many of these, especially the mutual societies, specifically preached thrift to the working classes. In the United States particularly, but also in the United Kingdom, thrift societies began to crop up. Henry Duncan, the son and grandson of Scottish Presbyterian ministers, founded the savings bank movement, influenced by Scottish Enlightenment thinkers, in particular the moral philosophy of Dugald Stewart, who he studied with at the University of Edinburgh. Charles Sikes founded the national system of postal savings banks in Britain, promoting penny banks and publishing a book entitled *Good Times, or The Savings Bank and the Fireside* (1854).

In addition, in both Britain and America, the YMCA, American Bankers Association, US Chambers of Commerce and many others celebrated National Thrift Week on an annual basis from 1917 onwards. In America, by the middle of the 1920s, a fully-fledged National Thrift Movement existed, aiming to teach Americans the 'Ten Commandments of Thrift'. However, Yates and Hunter argue that this movement was in effect a last attempt to keep classic thrift alive, in the face of other more popular forms of thrift that were very much breaking through. Effectively, they see it as 'classic thrift's grand finale' in the face of the 'consumer thrift' that was taking hold due to urbanisation, industrialisation and the expansion of the credit economy at the turn of the twentieth century (2011:22).

Neo-Victorians and household economia

When Theresa May took over as leader of the UK Conservative Party and prime minister, she referred to herself as a One Nation Conservative in her first speech, in which she outlined her focus on social justice.[16] Fellow Conservative MP and ex-mayor of London, Boris Johnson, has also spoken of his One Nationism, stating in 2010, 'I'm a one-nation Tory. There is a duty on the part of the rich to the poor and to the needy, but you are not going to help people express that duty and satisfy it if you punish them fiscally so viciously that they leave this city and this country'.[17] This link between Benjamin Disraeli's original One Nationism, and various iterations of Toryism that have followed since is of course well-understood and documented.[18] As British prime minister twice between the years of 1868 and 1880, Disraeli first conceived of the idea in his political novel, *Sybil, or The Two Nations* (1845).[19] *Sybil* was effectively a warning about what Britain would become if it allowed itself to be increasingly divided into the 'two nations' of rich and poor as a result of the onset of industrialisation and the heightened inequality it brought (Disraeli, 2016). It was, in many ways, a classic Victorian text; a moral tale about haves and have-nots, hard work and social justice (although one that essentially failed in its mission to unite the classes by having its heroine discover she is an heiress, thus resolving the romantic dilemma of her relationship with the well-to-do Mr Egremont).

Disraeli disliked the individualism of his era, and emphasised the importance of social obligation, such as charitable giving and philanthropy. This was part of his paternalistic vision of society in which the working classes were seen to require the support of the establishment due to being part of an 'organic society' in which classes had natural obligations to one another (Heywood, 2007). Similar ideas became part of the sociological framework offered up by Talcott Parsons' functionalism in the twentieth century – the acceptance that society was, and would always be, naturally hierarchical.[20] For Disraeli, this was essentially an extension of the idea of 'noblesse oblige' – the obligation on the aristocracy to be generous and honourable. Despite these philosophical groundings, there was also a pragmatism behind Disraeli's thinking. He was keenly aware that it would appeal to the newly enfranchised male working classes who had been given the vote in the Reform Act of 1867. It also enabled him to portray the Liberal Party as selfish individualists (Dorey, 1995:17) and preside over a series of reforms focused on the creation of a benevolent, yet still hierarchical, society. Many of these original One Nation views can be seen in current times, and they are palatably behind the current take on thrift and frugality in the UK. For example, the Conservative Party's 2010 manifesto included a section entitled 'One World Conservatism', with David Cameron naming Disraeli as his favourite Conservative. In addition, Conservative political theorist Phillip Blond proposed a renewed version of One Nation conservatism (2009).

However, with its emphasis on helping those that are prepared to help themselves and reiterating a conceptual line between the deserving and undeserving poor, the current thrift is far more aligned to Samuel Smiles' version of One Nationism than that of Disraeli himself. Smiles believed passionately in the attempt to lessen the gap between rich and poor, and equally passionately that this was to come about through the individual efforts of the working man. Despite acknowledging the more nuanced aspects of his political stance, parallels between his rhetoric and that of the present-day UK Conservative Party (under both David Cameron and Theresa May) are un-ignorable. The emphasis on 'hard-working families' throughout the 2015 UK election campaign was extreme, with the phrase being repeated seemingly ad infinitum. As David McWilliam argues, this return to a concept of the 'deserving poor' was used to justify the rollback of benefits and services under the austerity programme, and was predicated on 'a neoliberal ideology that views unemployment and poverty as stemming from personal failings rather than the ways in which the free market has shaped British society since the election of Margaret Thatcher in 1979' (2016:42).

This line of thinking can most obviously be associated with Charles Murray's neo-Victorian argument that the welfare state has created a workshy, antisocial and dependent underclass, who need rousing from their laziness and squalor by a discipline and stability like that associated with the Victorian era (2015).[21] It can be witnessed in the many television formats that tapped into the austerity rhetoric, judging people on their spending habits, their household clutter, their attempts to live like celebrities or indeed their survival on benefits (see *Saints and Scroungers, Benefits Street, The Only Way is Essex, Right on the Money, Britain's Spending Secrets, Til Debt do us Part* ... the list goes on). The logic of such programmes has provided and retained the ideological rationale for welfare cuts which, ironically, despite an apparent adherence to One Nation politics have most harmed those with the least, for example the disabled and single parents, creating a more polarised society than previously existed. (Amongst others, both Bev Skeggs and Helen Wood, 2012, and Angela McRobbie, 2008, have looked at televisual representations of the working classes, particularly women, in terms of themes such as 'respectability'.) This is also perhaps an inevitable consequence of the decades that fell in between Disraeli's version of Toryism and the present day – decades that saw the introduction of free-market capitalism, and then from the mid-1970s onwards, the rise of the New Right in global conservative politics that led to the critique of Keynesian economics and welfarism.[22,23]

The notion of frugality as part of a road to economic freedom, which was so key to Smiles' thinking, ties in to the above, as seen in rhetoric that extols the virtues of a few years of reigning things in, in order to be comfortable again in the future. This is precisely the message that was conveyed by Cameron and Osborne in 2009. Similarly, the Irish government tapped into a Catholic sensitivity by talking of the 'clearing up after the party'/atoning for one's economic sins. Both could easily be relying upon an image of the older, bloated, Franklin, reclining in his wealth, following his earlier life of industry and frugality. This, apparently, is to be our reward for the current frugality, as individuals, and as a nation. The 'work now to play later' message is a large part of current austerity messaging. The question is not only, will the 'play later' part ever be available, but also, *who* has to work hard and be thrifty now and within which structures and logics?

4

Spiritual thrift: simplicity, sensuality and politics in Henry Thoreau

Thoreau's sensual thrift

So far, this book has explored how the concept of thrift, motivated by various religious and individualist concerns, moved increasingly further away from its etymological sense of thriving, and closer to a sense of frugality at various points throughout history. Arguably, this shift in the meaning of the concept is at another historical high with the austerity culture in many European countries following the 2008 financial crash. Certainly, political rhetoric around austerity in the UK since then has focused heavily on individual financial responsibility. In fact, most of the important figures or ideas around thrift in this book tend towards ideas of frugality. It has proven difficult to find a conception of thrift that maintains the sense of thriving in the original definition.

The version of thrift that is perhaps easiest to wrestle away from concerns about frugality or even 'proper' house-keeping, is Henry Thoreau's (1817–1862). Thoreau was born in Concord, Massachusetts, in 1817 into a family of modest means. He studied at Harvard, but evidence suggests he never formally gained his master's due to his refusal to pay the five-dollar fee.[1] After 'graduation', Thoreau returned to Concord where he met Ralph Waldo Emerson (1803–1882) through a mutual friend.[2] Emerson, twenty-seven years Thoreau's senior, saw himself as a paternal advisor to Thoreau; an inclination which often led him to patronise the latter. Despite this, Emerson's influence on Thoreau cannot be underestimated. Emerson introduced him to a wide circle of writers and thinkers, encouraging him to contribute essays and poems. It was through some of those he met in this circle, including Emerson himself of course, that Thoreau was introduced to transcendentalism,[3] ideas from which pervade much of his later work.

Emerson and others in his circle held that it was possible to transcend the physical and empirical in order to achieve spiritual insight. This insight was however, importantly, not gained through religious doctrine, but through personal intuition. Key to this personal intuition was nature, or rather, Nature with a capital N. This, according to Emerson in his 1836 book *Nature*, was an outward sign of the internal spirit, and expressed the 'radical correspondence of visible things and human thoughts'. This emphasis on nature was to prove fundamental to Thoreau's own philosophy and work, and provide what is perhaps the most telling of his works, published posthumously – *Wild Fruits* (2001). They endorsed in their lectures and writings a more spontaneous, liberating and romantic 'transcendental simplicity' in which frugality was a means to a higher end. This was typified by Emerson's statement that 'economy is a high, humane office, a sacrament, when its aim is grand; when it is the prudence of simple tastes, when it is practiced for freedom, or love, or devotion' (cited in Shi, 2007:133).

Thoreau wrote prolifically on a variety of subjects, including natural history, philosophy and pressing issues of his day such as slavery.[4] However, it is *Walden*, his account of a year-long experiment in simple living which he embarked upon on 4 July 1845, which he is now best known for.[5] Despite selling disappointingly in his own lifetime, since Thoreau's death, *Walden* has become a celebrated classic, providing inspiration for many people wanting to escape what they feel to be their over-complicated lives and find a way of living that provides more space and time in which to experience the things they enjoy most. The book has also spawned a huge volume of academic articles and books, the synthesis of which would not be useful here. Instead, what follows attempts to look specifically at Thoreau's rationale for thrifty living; his political and spiritual motivations, and provide some historical context for them, in order to analyse what might be gleaned from them today.

In 1845 Thoreau built a small wooden hut on land owned by Emerson on the shores of Walden Pond (see figure 4.1). As detailed early on in *Walden*, the hut measured 'ten feet wide by fifteen long'; it had 'a garret and a closet, a large window on each side, two trap doors, one door at the end, and a brick fireplace opposite' (2012:28). He lived there, eating only from the land, bathing in the pond, making his own clothes, reading and contemplating nature. In its most simplistic form, this amounts to taking Thoreau's call to restore one's life to the 'simplicity' of a more primitive agricultural era head on, in order that it might be reduced to essentials, and the energy previously wasted on superfluities used to develop oneself spiritually. 'Simplify, simplify', Thoreau asserted, 'instead of three meals a day, if it be necessary, eat but one; instead of a hundred dishes, five; and reduce other things in proportion' (1985:395). This straightforward asceticism, however, needs to be viewed in the context of a spiritual interpretation of Thoreau, as what follows will explain.

Thoreau's famous quote explaining his decision to go to Walden is worth repeating at some length here:

4.1 Thoreau's cabin as drawn by his sister Sophia for the original title page of *Walden*

I went to the woods because I wished to live deliberately, to front only the essential facts of life, and see if I could not learn what it had to teach, and not, when I came to die, discover that I had not lived. I did not wish to live what was not life, living is so dear; nor did I wish to practise resignation, unless it was quite necessary. I wanted to live deep and suck out all the marrow of life, to live so sturdily and Spartan-like as to put to rout all that was not life, to cut a broad swath and shave close, to drive life into a corner, and reduce it to its lowest terms, and, if it proved to be mean, why then to get the whole and genuine meanness of it, and publish its meanness to the world; or if it were sublime, to know it by experience, and be able to give a true account of it in my next excursion.
(Thoreau, in *Walden*, 2012:51)

For Thoreau, living 'deliberately' was about the emptying out of inner lives as part of an inclination to find one's own inner spirituality. This was born very much out of transcendentalism, and like many transcendentalists of the day, this spirituality was influenced by Eastern philosophy. Thoreau was a keen reader of Eastern philosophy and it had considerable influence on him. *Walden* contains many references to sacred Indian texts. For example, he relates how he spends his mornings reading the Bhagavad Gita, and then equates the pond to the Ganges river, saying, 'I go to my well for water, and lo! there I meet the servant of the Brahmin, priest of Brahma and Vishnu and Indra … come to draw water for his master, and our buckets as it were grate together in the same well. The pure Walden water is mingled with the sacred water of the Ganges' (2012:161).

In particular, the mutual admiration between Gandhi and Thoreau is well documented but important to mention here. Dilip Nachane argues that one can see the influence of various thinkers in Gandhi's work, including Marx's emphasis on the exploitation of labour and class conflict (although violent revolution was anathema to him); Tolstoy's belief in the efficiency of truth and non-violence; and Ruskin's doctrine that the wealth of a nation consisted in its people not its products. However, Nachane insists that, first and foremost, Gandhi was influenced by the pastoral romanticism of Thoreau, along with his firm belief in non-violent civil disobedience (n.d.:S7).

In addition, like Thoreau, and unlike so many purveyors of thrift, there is a presentism in Gandhi's work, and in his fundamental motives for thrift. Furthermore, this presentism is precisely what makes Gandhi and Thoreau's thrift about thriving as much as it is about frugality, or to put it more accurately, frugality is a means to thriving in the present, rather than being financially sound in the future (as in Smiles or Franklin's version). As Nachane argues, 'Gandhi's views may seem somewhat similar to the Protestant ethics of thrift but with this crucial difference that with the latter thrift was a means of capital accumulation for higher consumption levels in the future, whereas for Gandhiji frugality was a permanent desired state, not simply a postponement of present for higher consumption' (Nachane, n.d.:S20).

Most crucially though, both Gandhi and Thoreau had a deep reverence for frugality and asceticism which they linked to the *spiritual development* of humankind, believing the latter was not attainable without leading an ascetic life. As Bhrigupati Singh attests, both Gandhi and Thoreau were conceptually and practically preoccupied with the ascetic ideal for most of their adult life (2010:7). For Gandhi this was via Brahmacharya (self-control or 'control of the passions') – hence his fasting and his celibacy. In Gandhi's book *Self-Restraint versus Self-Indulgence*, he included an appendix which was a short piece by Thoreau entitled 'Chastity and Sensuality' (Cavell, 1928), in which the latter says 'if it is the result of pure love, there can be nothing sensual in marriage. Chastity is something positive not negative. All lusts or base pleasures must give place to loftier delights' (Cavell, 1922:209).

As Singh acknowledges, numerous commentators have argued that sexuality is simply sublimated into nature in *Walden* (for example, Harding, 1991), but Singh says this is an impoverished view of the human, in which the human is forced into being distinct from nature – a view from which Thoreau is precisely trying to escape from (2010:8). As Singh argues, if we understand sensuality as heightened sense-perception then no book is more sensual than *Walden* (2010:8). Max Oelschlaeger agrees, emphasising Thoreau's intuitive understanding of nature through his immersion in it and arguing that his was a holistic approach – an 'Indian Wisdom' (1991:170). Victor Friesen, too, talks of Thoreau's immersion in the natural world and how he craves 'the experience of a sensual drenching … whether the place be forest or shoreline, whether the time be morning or evening, summer or winter'. He points to how Thoreau wanted to confine his mind in order to more experience his senses (1984:12). Finally, in *The Senses of Walden*, 1970s authority on Thoreau, Stanley Cavell, was entreating the reader of *Walden* to use the text as a guide in order to live deeper and suck out all of life's marrow (1922). Acknowledging the sensuality of Thoreau's thrift then, is a relatively well-trodden path, but no less important as a result.

Thoreau's asceticism was extreme, and could easily look puritanical at first glance, but running through it was a sense of the desire to get back to a sensory enjoyment of nature that the machinations of life under capitalism had somehow destroyed. Temperatures, tastes, textures, sounds, smells, tiny details of plants were all to be celebrated in Thoreau's version of thrift – a version we might usefully label sensual asceticism. Talking of village life, for example, he says, 'to wade sometimes in marshes where the bittern and the meadow-hen lurk, and hear the booming of the snipe; to smell the whispering sedge where only some wilder and more solitary fowl builds her nest' (2012:170–171). Talking of existence, he says, 'be it life or death, we crave only reality. If we are really dying let us hear the rattle in our throats and feel cold in the extremities' (2012:55). Indeed, Thoreau brings a delicious sensuality into the practice of thrift; for him frugality enabled a mode of heightened pleasure. This was a feature most adamantly held at bay by the puritanical purveyors of thrift and indeed most other adherents throughout history.

Thoreau's anti-capitalism

If, for Thoreau, living 'deliberately' was about finding a more spiritual way of living and being in touch with one's life, then it was also about re-gaining freedom and *time* not possible under the constraints of capitalism; time to live in a way that allowed him to notice the things around him and find joy in them. In other words, not to be weighed down by the necessity to earn and to have no choice but to take part in activities in everyday life that he did not wish to spend his time engaged in. His asceticism therefore may have been primarily driven by spiritualism, but was bound up in the ways that capitalism, *specifically*, disenabled such spiritualism. Luxuries, for Thoreau, were indeed positive hindrances to the spiritual elevation of mankind, but forsaking them was also about taking back the time required under capitalism to earn money for luxuries. In *Walden* he states, 'the cost of a thing is the amount of what I will call life which is required to be exchanged for it immediately or in the long run' (2012:18). Singh's interpretation of this is useful here. He argues 'the political salience of frugality for Thoreau is as a precondition for refusing allegiance to an objectionable state' (i.e. of capitalism), and describes *Walden* as an invitation to live a life of self-emancipation, 'lived without necessitating slavery' (Singh, 2010:17).

In fact, the minimalisation and indeed transformation of work and its place in the schema of everyday life is what drives Thoreau's thrift. Early on in his career he writes disparagingly of the factory system, saying 'I cannot believe that our factory system is the best mode by which men may get clothing. The condition of the operatives is becoming every day more like that of the English; and … as far as I have heard or observed, the principal object is, not that mankind may be well and honestly clad, but, unquestionably, that corporations may be enriched' (1985:343). Indeed, the first chapter of *Walden* provides economic context in a style not altogether dissimilar to Marx's *Capital*. Thoreau lists exactly how much each element of his house cost him: – 'Boards – $8.03; Lathes – $1.25; Two second-hand windows with glass – $2.43' and so on (2012:196).

Singh asks whether the huge amount of accounting detail and emphasis on frugality in Thoreau's first chapter can be likened to Franklin, but thankfully concludes that, in agreement with Cavell, Thoreau is probably using this listing exercise as a literary device to prove the pointlessness of such accounting (2010:11). Cavell, in typically dramatic style, puts it thus: 'For that is the obvious origin or locus of the use of economic imagery to express, and correct, spiritual confusion: what shall it profit a man; the wages of sin; the parable of talents; laying up treasures; rendering unto Caesar; charity. What we call the Protestant Ethic, the use of worldly loss and gain to symbolize heavenly standing, appears in *Walden* as some last suffocation of the soul. America and its Christianity have become perfect, dreamlike literalizations or parodies of themselves' (1922:88). Lance Newman, too, sees Thoreau's opening chapter as framing a critique of capitalism (2004:111), whilst, in an aligned argument, Richard Grusin argues that Thoreau borrows the language of market exchange in order to subvert, in doing so making the case that nature's economy is one of extravagant interconnection (1993).

Behind this framing of capitalism is a concern that the inner lives of people are being emptied out; that they 'are so occupied with the factitious cares and superfluously coarse labors of life that its finer fruits cannot be plucked by them' (Thoreau, 2012:4). However, it become clear how the spiritual and the material, or the ability to live spiritually and the constraints of capitalism, are bound together for Thoreau, as, for him, this emptying out occurs precisely due to the constraining effects of the web of economic relationships within which people are embroiled. There are also echoes of Veblen here, as Thoreau describes the way in which competitive social relations based on acquisition and display of status causes people to become 'slave-drivers' of themselves – a process set in motion by the ruling class. Thoreau's issue here is with class differentiations in general, but more specifically with the time and labour required to achieve the fineries that prove one's status, and the participation in an economic system based on exploitation (2012).

Clearly, the material and spiritual are both present in Thoreau's critique, and in the interpretations of those who analyse his work. For example, Leo Marx argues that Thoreau's criticism of the Concord way is, at its basis, not political. It is not the material or social conditions of life, i.e. not capitalism, that he feels causes the desperation of the masses, but their own spiritual inertia (Marx, 1964:32). So whilst he occasionally raises the issue of unequal access to social resources as part of this argument, Thoreau's point is not to encourage redistribution. His main concern about the state of the society around him is that it breeds not material but spiritual and intellectual poverty (Marx, 1964:33). Similarly, Newman argues that Thoreau directs his criticism at the influence of greed of the middle and upper classes, making the object of concern for him not the working class, but the 'potentially salvageable bourgeois slave driver of himself, who single-mindedly pursues material wealth and disregards the duty to the poor' (Newman, 2003:527).

Whilst these points are valid to an extent, it is important to recognise that the kinds of workers Thoreau speaks of as slave-driving themselves are not bourgeois necessarily, and he does acknowledge that the working classes have no time for themselves due to the control of capitalists. Therefore, he *is* blaming their spiritual inertia on the capitalist system they are trapped in, not on them per se. That he focuses on the bourgeoisie in terms of their spiritual lacking is undeniable, but this is not due to a lack of concern with redistribution, but rather that redistribution is not his major concern because he wants an alternative system from capitalism altogether. In this sense, he not a reformist, but a revolutionary. It's just that the revolution starts with himself, so is not easily readable as a classic revolutionary message.

It is perhaps also the case that Thoreau, in criticising capitalism, is criticising a wider logic that could be attributed to capitalism but that is also a more laterally connected issue – the logic of progress and the striving for a (apparent) good life that he feels has not been carefully enough examined or questioned. This comes through most clearly in his comments about the nation, worth repeating at some length here:

> Men think that it is essential that the Nation have commerce and export ice, and talk through a telegraph, and ride thirty miles an hour … If we do not get out sleepers and forge rails, and devote days and nights to the work, but go tinkering upon our lives to improve them, who will build railroads? And if railroads are not built, how shall we get to heaven in season? But if we stay at home and mind our business, who will want railroads? We do not ride on the railroad; it rides upon us. Did you ever think what those sleepers are that underlie the railroad? Each one is a man, an Irishman, or a Yankee man. The rails are laid on them, and they are covered with sand, and the cars run smoothly over them … some have the pleasure of riding a rail, others have the misfortune to be ridden upon. (From *Walden*, 2012:52)

Here Thoreau shows how against the development of the trainlines he was of course, but this is also a blistering critique of capitalism with its collateral damage and winners and losers and provides a deep questioning of the goals and assumptions behind 'progress'. It is a critique of what Thoreau sees as a needless, irrational development, a Faustian development, which does not consider why it is necessary or what it is achieving (and of course for whom). Thoreau's simplicity then is not just about living plainly; it is about a wider questioning of improvement and development and a plea in many ways to reconsider the rationale for development and therefore the entire idea of a better life.

It is important to note that this interpretation of Thoreau as anti-capitalist more or less adheres to the traditionalist interpretation of his work in which he is portrayed as what one might these days call a green anti-capitalist. The revisionist interpretation argues that Thoreau was not entirely dis-embedded from the process of capitalism in place in his day and that his sojourn at Walden can be seen as entrepreneurial and driven by a sense of entrepreneurial ability to survive in the wild. The issue with this revisionist version is that Thoreau himself did not see his survival in and via nature and its products as an experiment in making a living, but rather in making a life. Revisionist accounts are perhaps unable to step outside the capitalist thinking of *their own* times, hence interpreting Thoreau as unable to step outside of his.

As previously mentioned, much like his spiritual views, Thoreau's political views also intersected with those of Gandhi. The political influence between them is well known and much written about, in particular the concept of satyagraha.[6] Although Gandhi discovered satyagraha before he had read Thoreau, the latter had a tremendous impact on its further development.[7] Gandhi was influenced by Thoreau's essay 'Life without Principle' (a critique of the excesses of nineteenth-century capitalism), and of course not least by his celebrated essay 'The Duty of Civil Disobedience'.[8] Both were required reading in Gandhi's Ashram. Some commentators have perhaps rather simplistically interpreted Thoreau's civil disobedience essay as an anarchist text, and it is certainly the case that Thoreau's ideas have resonated with various anarchist strains. Green anarchism and anarcho-primitivism in particular have taken inspiration from the writings of Thoreau. Additionally, Murray Rothbard, the founder of anarcho-capitalism, considers Thoreau one of the movement's greatest intellectual heroes. Thoreau was also an important influence on late nineteenth-century anarchist naturism, and his ideas greatly informed individualist anarchist circles in Europe. However, there is actually little suggestion of abolishing government in Thoreau's essay; rather a plea to hold government to account in light of the will of the people. Thoreau's argument is that individuals should not permit governments to overrule their own consciences, and that they have a duty to disenable governments to make them the agents of injustice. He does not suggest that government in and of itself is an inappropriate form. This too is broadly in line with Gandhi's thinking.

Spiritual individualism versus material collectivism in Thoreau

Much has been written about the ways in which Thoreau's work shifts between spiritual and materialist concerns; or sensory asceticism and politically motivated asceticism (see, for example, James McIntosh's argument about

Thoreau's constantly shifting stance on nature). Running parallel to such debates over spiritualism and materialism are those concerned with Thoreau's individualism versus his collectivism. Indeed, his spiritualism is often posited as to blame for his individualism by those disappointed by what they perceive to be a lack of a more societal vision on the part of Thoreau. Allegations of extreme individualism are not without some evidence. Thoreau's first published political essay, 'Paradise (To Be) Regained', was a critique of Etzler's technological utopian manifesto, in which he argues against the mechanical thinking that informs Etzler's scheme, including its planned *collective* transformation of the material basis of human social relations.[9] Instead, he advocates self-reliance, as of course many transcendentalists did at the time. However, Thoreau's was a far more complicated mixture of transcendentalist individualism and materialist concerns with society, which the following section will attempt to unpick.

As Newman argues, Thoreau's intellectual development had begun in 'the thin atmosphere of Romantic idealism, with its sharp distinctions between spirit and matter, "man" and "nature", but over time he came to see the natural and social worlds as integrated and inseparable' (2004:105–106). It is important to recognise that this was within the context of the times, in which the existing idealist notion of creation was competing against the emergent materialist theory of evolution. Thoreau had been moving towards Darwin's argument throughout the 1850s, with the publication of his writing on scientific ecology such as 'The Dispersion of Seeds' and 'The Succession of Forest Trees' (now published as part of *Wild Fruits*). In 1859, he eagerly read Darwin's *Origin of Species* in 1859, as soon as it arrived in Concord. However, despite Darwin's considerable influence on him, Thoreau continued to think of nature as a divine creation in a material present. Newman puts it rather well, saying that Thoreau 'remained committed to the idealist notion of an active supernatural force driving natural processes, whilst at the same time his study of those processes, and the language he used to describe them, became increasingly materialist and empiricist' (2004:109–110).

In this way, Thoreau's thought was able to develop with idealism and materialism; transcendentalism and science; individualism and collective concerns, in parallel throughout much of his life, and many scholars have interpreted *Walden* as a complex choice between idealist and materialist interpretations and experiences of the world. As Newman points out, in *Walden* Thoreau provides detailed, representational accuracy in his descriptions of the woods around Concord, yet he also consistently speaks of natural facts as symbolic of human experience. In doing so, *Walden* 'articulates a moral critique of social relations under capitalism based on materialist analysis of economic relationships', but 'offers an idealist and individualist solution to this problem' (Newman, 2004:112).

Thoreau's attitude towards the experimental collective living arrangement at the nearby Brook Farm is an excellent practical indication of the way in which this path between individualism and collective social action played out.[10] Brook Farm was created by George Ripley, who came to prominence during the election campaigning of 1840, largely as he held appeal for Boston's reform-minded intellectuals following the political demise of Orestes Brownson.[11] His announcement that he intended to move to a small tract of land outside the city with a group of like-minded individuals was seen as galvanising Boston (Newman; 2004:521). The group aimed to build a self-sustaining cooperative that would function as a micro-society. Ripley felt that the immorality and greed of the wealth had caused social dislocation and that the increasingly entrenched hierarchy of the classes was essentially the result of judgements about the relative value of physical and intellectual labour. He therefore felt that those who engaged in intellectual labour, especially if they were leaders of the ruling classes as he was, ought to lead by example, and engage in manual labour as a form of revolutionary activity (Ripley, 2007). His aim was to create a more natural union between intellectual and manual labour in order to combine the thinker and the worker, as far as possible, in the same individual. In doing so, he hoped to 'guarantee the highest mental freedom, by providing all with labor, adapted to their tastes and talents and securing to them the fruits of their industry; to do away with the necessity of menial services, by opening the benefits of education and the profits of labor to all; and thus to prepare a society of liberal, intelligent, and cultivated persons, whose relations with each other would permit a more simple and wholesome life' (Ripley, 2007:16).

Ripley's motivating concerns were not at all dissimilar to those of Thoreau, and indeed were broadly similar to those of most transcendentalists (in fact Ripley invited Emerson to join him at Brook Farm). Theodore Parker's 'Thoughts on Labor' is very similar in argument to Ripley's on the idea of each man engaging in physical labour to provide for himself. Emerson too published similar thoughts in his 'Man the Reformer' which explains the doctrine of Brook Farm as every man standing 'in primary relations with the work of the world', and not suffering 'the accident of having a purse in his pocket ... to sever him from those duties' (1841:530). In fact, Newman argues the quest to return dignity and importance to physical labour preoccupied a remarkable number of the transcendentalists during the first years of the 1840s: Thoreau grew beans, Emerson became a gardener, and Bronson Alcott drew up his plan for the agricultural community Fruitlands (Newman, 2003:521–522).

However, once the Brook Farm group began their attempt they found it was very difficult to enable the farm to cover its costs, let alone make any profit, in the depressed economy of the day. As a result, they decided to look to the principles of the French utopian socialist Charles Fourier. Fourier's philosophy centred on three key concepts: (1) association, the principle of forming large communities or phalanxes in which the economies of scale could be applied to domestic arrangements; (2) attractive industry, the idea of organising labour around the propensities and abilities of the individual community members in order to make it pleasant; and (3) equality of compensation for capital and intellectual and manual labour. Once Brook Farm applied the principles of Fourierism, it began to grow rapidly and its character changed from 'a kind of barely self-sustaining retreat for a like-minded elite' into 'a burgeoning center of agricultural and industrial production' (Newman, 2003:525). A coach line was set up which enabled thousands of visitors to come from Boston each year, and turned the farm into a profit-making business. As a result, it came to be seen as the flagship of the national Association[12] movement and a number of Brook Farm residents started to promote the movement by delivering lectures throughout the north-east and the west (Newman, 2003:525).

It was this transformation of Brook Farm into a capitalistic business that Thoreau found so abhorrent, and that caused his robust criticism of it. For him, the experiment had fallen into the rationalisation of the market (Newman, 2003:533). As a result, Thoreau scaled back his own at Walden, sowing just a few rows for personal consumption and writing 'I will not plant beans and corn with so much industry another summer, but such seeds … as sincerity, truth, simplicity, faith, innocence, and the like' (Thoreau, 2012:90). Underneath Thoreau's actions was the desire to escape the constant calculations of profit and loss that he witnessed at Brook Farm, which he saw as a somehow false creation. As Newman says, 'he was repulsed by Brook Farm not because it was a community but because it was artificial. Intelligence with the earth, on the other hand, offered Thoreau an intuitive, an organic, means of connection with the laws of nature' (2003:534). This was not Thoreau asserting individualism against collectivism, but rather market contrivances against unaccountable means of survival.

Despite Thoreau and the Brook Farm members having a rather similar conception of what constituted 'the problem', then, and a shared conviction that the challenge was to find a way to reduce the amount of time necessary to earn a living through paid work, Thoreau's solution was to reduce his wants to a bare minimum and live this out through individual example, whereas Ripley's solution was to take advantages of economies of scale – a capitalistic device thrown up by the market. However, Thoreau was not unconcerned with collective action simply because his answer was to experiment on his own and indeed was not opposed to Brook Farm based on the fact it was collective, but rather due to its lack of resistance to the mechanisms of capitalism.

Certainly, at the beginning of *Walden*, 'Thoreau adopts such a cavalierly individualist position about how to respond' and is 'startlingly confident' in his ability to withdraw from the market (Newman, 2004: 113–114). However, for Newman, Thoreau's individualism in *Walden* 'is part of a confrontational, aggressive persona designed to startle his audience into new ways of thinking ... for the book's final goal is to engender wholesale social reform through individual acts of self-reform' (2004:114–115), and this is the sense in which Thoreau's version of thrift should be understood. Indeed, by the end of the 1850s, Thoreau's work had become much less concerned with individual spirituality (however broadly he may have defined that), and much more concerned with direct action that might be able to intervene in the course of history. He became increasingly concerned with issues of social justice, particularly slavery, and his collective concerns came to the fore as he gradually moved away from transcendental idealism. His later abolitionist essays provide proof of this. In fact, as Ding Zhaoguo argues, the significance of Thoreau's social and political thoughts lies precisely in his seeing a relationship between self-reform in individuals and wider social justice and political democracy (2008:37). Therefore, accusations that his primary concern was not for society but for the individual can be more usefully viewed within the context of his concern regarding the relationship between the individual and the State. It is within this context that his view on social reform being mainly realised through individual self-reform ought to be assessed.

Still the best account of Thoreau's radicalisation in response to economic and political developments in New England is Leo Stoller's *After Walden: Thoreau's Changing Views on Economic Man*, in which Stoller argues that Thoreau's ongoing negotiation between idealism and materialism gradually led to him preferring direct action as opposed to individualist principles alone (1957). For Stoller, the competing nature of individualism and collectivism throughout Thoreau's work, and the way in which by the end of his life they appeared to have become one, is typical of reformers at the time. He argues, 'America was entering a major depression. Each person had his unique problem to solve ...

But to the men and women called reformers the predicaments of the individual and of the nation seemed inseparable' (1957:1). The ideal therefore, according to Stoller, was 'self-culture'; life aimed at full realisation of every person's innate capacities (1957:4). This 'self-culture' was directly inspired by Unitarian thought, specifically the work of William Ellery Channing, who, according to Stoller, 'transmitted to a later and a different age the faith in human perfectibility which he had learned of the Enlightenment'. Channing believed all humans to be capable of perfection and, according to Stoller, elements of his doctrine are to be found 'scattered through the fragmentary journals of the late thirties and early forties', especially in his early essay 'The Service' (Stoller, 1957:4).

Stoller's argument, however, is that Thoreau took this ideal of Channing's and 'grafted it onto an economic stock of anti-industrialism and … a theory of social action suited to his own temperament' (1957:5). What this meant in practice was that Thoreau took the 'self-culture' part of Channing's doctrine, but refused to accept, as Channing did, that, because it was a matter for the individual, it was possible despite the social system of machines and profit, through the disciplined exploitation of one's spare time (1957:3). In fact, Thoreau became increasingly convinced of an incompatibility between 'self-culture' and a society based on the need to make profit; leisure and pay in return for labour was simply not enough to enable self-culture. This explains how Samuel Smiles had taken self-culture in such a different direction to Thoreau. In fact, given this information, it might be easy to conceive of Thoreau's interpretation of self-culture as more wayward than Smiles', rather than vice versa as previously suggested.

Wild Fruits and the promise of collectivism

Thoreau died aged forty-four in 1862, having contracted tuberculosis some years before, and then becoming ill with bronchitis. After his death, the manuscript for a book was found wrapped in a large sheet of paper upon which was written the title *Wild Fruits*.[13] It was from this manuscript that the essay 'Wild Apples' had been taken and sent to *Atlantic Monthly* a month before his death. *Wild Fruits* at first glance appears to be a botanical guide to the wild plants of New England, but is also visionary in its nature, convoking an organic community as an alternative to capitalism. It is incomplete and fragmentary, but Newman argues that despite this it 'clearly confirms the trajectory of Thoreau's traverse from idealism and individualism to materialism and communalism' (2004:116).

Certainly, his place in any 'history of thrift' should be viewed with his final posthumous work and the impact this has upon his legacy fully acknowledged.

Wild Fruits is a subtle and highly original synthesis of individualism and materialist concerns, in which issues of environmental and social justice formed the basis of a robust critique of capitalism and an underlying concern with collective transformation of ecological and social order. As Laura Walls puts it, Thoreau attempted 'to read and tell a history of man and nature together, as and in one single, interconnected act' (Walls, 1995:214). This synthesis posited natural and human history as parts of an integrated eco-social process. If Thoreau had previously been criticised for picking huckleberries alone, *Wild Fruits* saw him most definitely doing so as part of a community and is generally agreed to provide a blueprint for collective alternative living. The book sees Thoreau begin to envision a utopian alternative, in the form of an organic community living in daily communion with the land.

In fact, *Wild Fruits* enables us to read *Walden* as a work about individual transformation, but one which Thoreau in his later years saw as having the potential to trigger wider societal change. In many ways it removes the 'limit' Leo Stoller writes of when he argues that *Walden* was a work primarily concerned with individual, not social, reform because Thoreau saw his responsibility as ending once he had embodied the principle himself. He says, 'to become a squatter by the side of Walden Pond and there attempt to demonstrate the practicability of a subsistence economy as the foundation for self-culture was enough. If other men observed his success or listened to his descriptions of it and were convinced by his example, they were then free to follow' (Stoller, 1957:87). In the context of *Wild Fruits*, however, it is not unfair to argue that by the end of his life, Thoreau most certainly wanted all people to follow his personal example, and his was a living blueprint for a *collective* alternative to capitalism and indeed a thrift that gets closer to a sense of thriving than most other versions.

Walls' interpretation of *Wild Fruits* is one that most vehemently attests to its call for collective action, of the type that engages with nature in order to resist the capitalist market. She argues, 'themes of decline and fragmentation are countered with pleas for collective strength and achievement: these late "nature" essays are finally some of Thoreau's most social writing' (1995:213). By way of example, Walls takes Thoreau's description of individual grasses on a hillside that together give a purple effect, saying that for Thoreau 'fall [Autumn] becomes a celebration of collective identity, a utopian vision of the entire countryside as a flag of flags' (1995:215). Even more poignantly, and radically, she argues, the essay 'Wild Apples' likens the immigrant domestic apple tree to New World

Europeans, and their misuse (by the marketing and sale of them) signals the way America is bringing the evil days upon itself. Certainly, Thoreau laments the amount of land being made private, and the marketisation of various edible plants, mentioning how huckleberry pickers are being ordered out of the fields, and saying for example 'the era of the Wild Apple will soon be past. It is a fruit which will probably become extinct in New England ... I fear that he who walks over these fields a century hence will not know the pleasure of knocking off wild apples' (2001:250). He asks what the value of country life is, if one must go to market for it, and talks about how people are effectively permitting the huckleberries to be enslaved (2001:251). And then finally, as Walls points out, he offers a collective solution to these laments – that in each town there should be a committee that made sure the beauty of the town was protected and that natural beauty belonged to the public (1995:223).

Thoreau's version of simple living is without competition the most pervasive in current-day American culture, and quite possibly in other Anglophone parts of the world. It is *Walden* that is harked back to by those attempting to live simply and engage in thrift today. And his is a version of thrift very much about thriving. His politics on governance and the like were foundations that could not really have underlaid a more economically concerned version of thrift. His frugality was about touching spirituality and finding the ability to experience each moment of life – as he said, 'most of the luxuries, and many of the so-called comforts of life, are not only not indispensable, but positive hindrances to the elevation of mankind. With respect to luxuries and comforts, the wisest have ever lived a more simple and meagre life than the poor' (Thoreau, 2012:9). It is important to acknowledge that Thoreau himself was privileged, not only in his own status as a white, middle-class man, but also in that through knowing Emerson it was possible for him to build a hut on land without being evicted, and to live off that land. His was a form of voluntary rural austerity. For him, and many intellectuals influenced by transcendentalism (including those who were part of the Brook Farm experiment), the choice was avowedly agricultural. They did not choose to make shoes or engage in industrial collectivity, but rather remained utterly faithful to agrarian collectivity, largely because they believed that through dealing directly with nature, one could access one's inner spirituality. Yet despite his position of relative luxury, and the determined emphasis on the rural that pervades his work, Thoreau's politics can be taken seriously, and make his version of thrift far more radical than most, and far closer to an idea of what a thrift concerned with thriving might look like.

5

Nationalist thrift: making do, rationing and nostalgic austerity

'Make do and mend': thrift in the name of democracy

So far, this book has tackled the religious thrift of the Puritans with its Providentialist and later more pragmatic concerns, the strict moral thrift of the Victorians with its grounding in individualism and social righteousness, and the spiritual individualism and communal vision of Thoreau. This chapter will explore examples of thrift quintessentially different from those witnessed so far, due to their emphasis on social solidarity based not on a religious faith, as with the Puritans, or on a strict moral code, as with the Victorians, or even on a spirit of self-discovery such as with Thoreau, but on a new and powerful grounding – that of the fight for national survival.

The thrift of the British populace during the Second World War is one of the strongest examples of frugality carried out in the national interest. Between 1940 and 1955 rationing was in place in Britain, gradually easing off as more and more products became available again following the end of the war in 1945. It was necessary due to changes in food production and supply that had taken place prior to the war beginning – much land was changed to pasture and animals were fed on imported fodder (Gardiner, 2004). Under the Emergency Powers Act the Ministry of Agriculture could requisition farms, intervene wherever farm production was unsatisfactory, and control the slaughter of livestock and the price offered to producers. In addition, Ministry of Information publications encouraged 'digging for victory' (see figure 5.1) – a large-scale campaign launched to encourage people to grow more food on allotments (Hinton and Redclift, 2009:12–13). By 1942 it was estimated that over half Britain's manual workers had an allotment or were growing food in their garden (Gardiner, 2004:166).[1]

It was not only food that required careful management. The Second World War in Britain also saw the launch of various government poster campaigns advocating thrift in other areas of everyday life, in a determined effort to drive down the consumptive needs of the population. Ministry of Information

5.1 'Dig for victory' poster from the Second World War

publications gave tips on how to save on household items from string to electricity, and encouraged people to 'Make do and Mend' when it came to clothes (see figure 5.2). A series of posters and pamphlets set out to provide useful tips to housewives on how to be both frugal and stylish in times of strict

5.2 'Make do and mend' poster from the Second World War

clothes rationing (1941 until 1949). Via the character of Mrs Sew-and-Sew, these publications emphasised how crucial it was not to consume materials and commodities one could do without, and how to elongate the use-value of an item of clothing by darning, reinforcing and re-using in a different capacity. Readers were advised to create 'decorative patches', to unpick old jumpers in order to re-knit chic alternatives, and to turn men's clothes into women's.

Waste too was an important factor, with regular collections for different types of waste that could be used in the war effort – scrap metal for weapons, food scraps for pig fodder. In many ways the Second World War saw the beginnings of a recycling sector that is well-established in Britain today and cemented generational attitudes towards the wasting of anything. (In fact, one of the great generational divides of the 1960s was that the younger generation were seen as horrifically wasteful in the eyes of their parents, causing an array of preachy books typified by Vance Packard's 1970 publication, *The Waste Makers*.)

Government campaigns were not the only way in which messages of thrift got to the British people; they also became embedded in popular media of the time. Ballaster *et al.* claim women's magazines became a key way to disseminate information and boost morale (1991:110). For obvious reasons, this thrift was essentially a far more collective endeavour than that from various other historical moments. As Winship notes, articles that addressed thrift in women's magazines of the time tended strongly to foreground the nation's needs over those of the individual and family (1987:31). It is worth noting, however, that despite the collective emphasis in this thrift, elements of consumer thrift also came through. For example, as Waller and Vaughan-Rees argue, despite the strong emphasis on 'making do', there was also a very prevalent advertising theme in UK magazines which insisted all products were needed 'more than ever before' (1987:94). According to Waller and Vaughan-Rees, then, the war was used to sell products, just as much as it advocated consumer restraint. Similarly, Parkin studied the content of American Second World War adverts and found an interrelation between frugality and consumption (2006). She notes how US companies typically encouraged consumers to buy their products by claiming that their product was economical and patriotic (2006:9495).

Radio too was an important means of dissemination of wartime thrift. In Britain, Mrs Mopp, a character in the radio comedy *It's That Man Again* – or *ITMA* as it became fondly known – became symbolic of the many women left in bombed-out urban areas, surviving against the odds, unglamorous and immune to frivolity, but with a stoicism that was a vital part of saving the nation.[2] Mrs Mopp, played by Dorothy Summers, was an office cleaner with the catchphrase

'Can I do yer now Sir?'[3] She appeared in a special wartime record to advertise British Gas and Electricity and advise on conserving energy supplies, in which she is advised by Mayor Handley '*You* must be the home guard you old flap-duster ... this [government] letter says we've all got to be care-fuel, I'm sorry I mean careful. Every bit of gas we save in the home means more gas and coal to make munitions in the factories ... guard against waste and you'll be making munitions in your own home'. 'What? Me making munitions sir?' she asks. 'Yes, you and me and everybody else, just by saving gas and other fuels.' Mayor Handley then goes on to give advice such as 'put on two pairs of winter woolies and do without a gas fire ... never wash up under a running tap ... use less water in your bath ... and don't use the oven for only one dish – that's slap-ovenry. Do you understand?' To which Mrs Mopp meekly replies, 'I've got the idea sir'. She does have some recourse to challenge, however, as true to her dour and somewhat judgemental character, towards the conclusion of the sketch she asks 'But what about you sir? What about the time you waste when you're supposed to be in conference, with your feet stuck up on the mantelpiece, warming yourself in front of the gas fire, and the times you leave it blazing away when you nip round the corner?' 'Alright Mrs Mopp it's a bargain' comes the response. 'I'll do my bit and you do yours and I hope everybody else will follow suit.'[4]

This 'doing one's bit' was, according to Hinton and Redclift, part of a deeper voluntaristic tradition of the nation (2009:14). However, there was something specifically domestic about this volunteerism when it came to Second World War thrift in Britain. Nationalism entered the home as part of a powerful wartime rhetoric and thrift was more poignantly than ever about household economia. As Gardiner argues, rationing and the government campaigns on making do brought the battle front into the home, and made women particularly a 'front line' in the war effort (2004: 181). A saucepan could become a spitfire.

Characters such as Mrs Mopp and Mrs Sew-and-Sew are proof of the extent to which the wartime version of thrift became deeply embedded in British society. In many ways, they re-harnessed certain elements of Smiles' conception of thrift, such as his emphasis on good self-management and personal propriety. Only this time, crucially, the emphasis on personal responsibility was not about saving money for the future, or to guard against future tough times, as it was for Smiles' ideal citizen, but rather about saving *resources* in order that the nation would be able to maintain the battle for a far grander cause – 'our values'. With the onset of war, thrift became rooted in the desire to fend off an external enemy that threatened values perceived as 'ours' – such as freedom and democracy. Thrift during the Second World War was about solidarity through collectivity specifically to fight against the fascism of Hitler's Germany. It was at this time, therefore, *only* about collectivity and solidarity in order to fight for a larger concept; it was not about solidarity *for its own sake*, which is almost certainly why it returned to an individualistic version of itself so quickly after the end of the war.

Self-sufficiency was engineered by necessity in wartime, and the British people became used to scarcity and having their consumptive choices, even on basic food products, administered from above (see Sissons and French, 1964; Longmate, 1971; Briggs, 1975; Hennessy, 1993).[5] Wartime propaganda campaigns emphasised that personal sacrifices would ultimately contribute to military victory. This victory was nationalist not only in a straightforward sense that it was about a nation winning, but also in the sense that it defined the nation as the thing that could protect other, larger, less tangible and extremely important qualities – namely democracy.

This brief period of collective thrift was not exclusive to Britain. In the United States, 'defense saving bonds' were re-named 'war bonds' after Pearl Harbor, but were popular before the attack too. In fact, from 1941 to 1956 eight out of thirteen Americans invested in war bonds (Adatto, 2011:380). Kiku Adatto argues that in the United States the Second World War provided a 'dramatic example of thrift collectively conceived' and points to how it was positioned as being for the greater good (2011:380). The development of collective thrift through the social attempt to serve the greater good meant that saving money was directly equated to serving the nation as part of the war effort.

Here, too, democracy was the uniting factor. Thrift was put to the service of democracy in that it was part of a war fought for democratic ideals that everyone could participate in by joining in the society-wide thrift movement (Adatto, 2011:399). Roosevelt saw savings bonds in particular as tokens of partnership with the old world that would perpetuate democracy in the new world and aid the democracy that was under threat in the old world. As Adatto argues, the war bonds were about unity through diversity, and the common goal of democracy. In this sense they differed from both the 'liberty bonds' issued during the First World War, which had been much more simplistically patriotic and had often spoken to a white, Anglo-Saxon, Protestant American citizen, and from the shallow nationalism of the patriotic bonds issued after 9/11 (2011:381). In contrast, the war bonds of the Second World War were decidedly inclusive in their appeal. For example, William Pickens was chosen to coordinate the war bond campaigns in African-American communities and 'negro savings clubs' sprung up particularly in the South.

War bonds were promoted as 'an obligation of citizenship, as a way of honoring the sacrifices of America's fighting men, and as an expression of national and intergenerational solidarity' (Adatto, 2011:383). Campaigns to encourage take-up of war bonds were organised door-to-door and in workplaces, via the 'minute men' and 'minute women' who were known as 'victory volunteers', as well as through national media campaigns and Hollywood (stars such as Humphrey Bogart and Betty Grable). Adatto says, 'the war bond campaign was conceived and run as a people's campaign. It enlisted the power of sentiment to inspire civic action and lifted sentimentality from its familiar habitation in private life and infused it with civic purpose' (2011:385). There was, therefore, a 'homeyness' to the campaign, not dissimilar to Roosevelt's 'fireside chats' and his insistence that each family was part of a common defence, not just the soldiers. Indeed, Roosevelt harked back to Lincoln in his campaign, using his image on many of the promotional campaign posters, along with his famous words from the Gettysburg address, 'a government of the people, by the people, for the people shall not perish on this earth'.

A domestification of thrift was part of the US message, just as it was in the UK. Part of this domestication was the role of children, who were also asked to see themselves as 'soldiers' – creating school 'victory gardens' in the United States, and collecting waste and pig fodder in the UK. Robert Merton argues that people were motivated to buy war bonds by a spirit of sacrifice that was fundamentally about families 'back home' sacrificing something just as the soldiers were doing (1947). Certainly, the bonds were hung on a powerful rhetoric of blood, suffering and national unity, with very little actual explanation of how exactly the bonds and the soldiers related to one another, or how the bonds would help win the war or bring the soldiers home. It is perhaps telling that in the United States, the real point of these savings bonds was to help soak up the 'wild money' that the government felt people had during the war because there was nothing to spend it on once rationing began in the United States (Adatto, 2011:382). After the war, the 'good for America' part of the ad campaigns for national bonds became just the last in a long list of far more individualistic reasons to invest.

Second World War nostalgia and the cupcake revolution

The focus on 'cutting back' and taking individual and household responsibility was pushed to the forefront of news agendas and everyday life in Britain from 2009 onwards alongside a sudden wave of Second World War nostalgia. Despite being essentially neo-Victorian as discussed in the previous chapter, the rhetoric and branding of this new austerity vociferously utilised imagery and sentiments surrounding the Second World War. In fact, it would not be unfair to suggest that this nostalgia was triggered and encouraged by institutions aligned to the government's stance in order to help sell the idea of a new austerity to the British populace. Indeed, as various commentators have argued, it is the Second World War era that has mainly been used in the actual social encouragement of frugality in the name of austerity (see Hinton and Redclift, 2009; Randall, 2009; Ginn, 2012). Much of this nostalgia was fed by the Imperial War Museum's 'Wartime Spirit' campaign which reissued the 1943 pamphlet 'How to Make Do and Mend', which urged the British public to 'make do and mend', 'walk short distances', 'save fuel for battle', 'save kitchen scraps to feed the pigs', 'don't waste water', 'waste paper is still vital', 'dig for victory', 'holiday at home', 'eat greens for health' and 'keep calm and carry on'. The last of these tagline – 'keep calm and carry on' has become an increasingly ubiquitous sign everywhere in Britain since 2009.

However, Bramall argues that the myth of the home front enables the Second World War to function more generally as a powerful rhetorical device. Certainly, popular cultural references of wartime Britain are very effective vehicles for current austerity policies. In particular, the 'make do and mend' slogan has re-gained resonance, now however conjuring cosy images of wartime solidarity, and retro renditions of the wartime tagline 'keep calm and carry on' are in plentiful supply.[6] Mugs incite us to 'keep calm and have a brew', toilet lids to 'keep calm and take a seat', cushions to 'keep calm and take a nap'. Such items are part of a resurgence in the popularity of ideas of home-making and simplicity that has also seen sales for retro kitchen appliances (typically the KitchenAid food mixer) increase, and the popularity of 'home-baking' (typically in the form of the cupcake) take on epidemic levels.[7] National organisations also got in on the act. In April 2009, the UK's Energy Saving Trust launched a 'war time spirit' campaign to encourage people to save money and energy in response to recession and climate change.[8] It is no coincidence that these things are associated with the housewife of the 1940s; the scrimping and saving, head-scarfed and rosy-cheeked heroine of the home front. As Clarke and Newman argue, austerity in the UK today necessarily invites echoes of that earlier postwar austerity by dint of the existence of a collective memory of rationing, making do and mending, and a culture of restraint (2012). But there is more at play here than simple collective memory. There is also a wilful play upon that memory – a politically and ideologically charged intent to connect the two eras – as evidenced by British Prime Minister David Cameron's initial use of the phrase 'age of austerity', and Chancellor George Osborne's now famous 'we are all in this together' speech in 2009.[9,10]

When Cameron used the phrase 'age-of-austerity' it was by way of a comparison to an apparent previous era that he referred to as an age of 'irresponsibility'. In doing so he therefore connected austerity to responsibility, and it is from this mindset that the current ideologies of thrift have emerged. To be thrifty is to be responsible, and as 'we are all in this together' as citizens of a nation state, it is to be responsible as a nation citizen, and specifically as an economic citizen. Thrift then, in the current austerity, is a pervasive mix of nationalism, economic individualism and moralism, *promoted* as collective interest and a return to some kind of nostalgic 'simplicity' that never existed. In reality, this austerity is a long way from being collective or simple. Indeed, as Clarke and Newman argue, 'this is the collective imagery that the Coalition has tried to summon up – a nation united in the face of adversity' (2012:303). A nation whose support is garnered by the creation of a sense of the absolute necessity to avert disaster by everyone pulling together – *as if* there were an external enemy on our shores – hence the success of appealing to wartime campaigns of thrift and collective effort.

Indeed, in an article for the *Guardian* in 2010, historian David Kynaston offered a comparative account of the two austerities. He argued that creating the political will for austerity among a postwar public was 'a hard sell then' but is considerably harder in the present. He traced four conditions that had enabled postwar austerity to command popular assent (although not enthusiastic support): a sense of shared purpose, a perceived equity of sacrifice, an aura of hope and a degree of public confidence in the political class. Similarly, Hinton and Redclift argue that this conflation of two very different periods of economic hardship disguises many of the differences between the two situations, provides mythical portrayals of 'Blitz spirit' and overlooks the fact that after the war, consumption and consumerism increased markedly – leading to the problems we confront today (2009:5). It is these same conditions that Cameron and Osborne attempted to garner, despite the fact that, as Clarke and Newman quite correctly point out, they seem rather less reliable in the present day. At best, the purpose of austerity is 'shared on a sort of grudging acquiescence about the condition of the global economy, the public debt and the "necessity" of tough measures' (2012:307). It is not dissimilar to Margaret Thatcher's claim that 'There Is No Alternative' (TINA), which typically evoked grudging compliance rather than enthusiastic support.

This 'anti-consumerist' bent, traditionally the preserve of the left, has been taken on by commentators on the political left and right, largely due to a lack of clarity as to whether such practices ought to be seen as permanent (typically the attitude of the Left), or part of a temporary phase that will enable a return to full consumerism. Alan Bradshaw puts forward Ireland as an interesting case study of the latter, arguing that austerity measures have been put to the Irish populace as a form of 'repentance' that must be undergone following the 'sins' of the 'party' (i.e. the wild era of the rise of the Celtic Tiger). He argues that in the context of a Catholic country, the propensity of the people to feel guilt is played upon, enabling austerity measures to be understood as the 'hail Marys' of a nation confessing in order to return to its previous state of being (Bradshaw, 2019). Similarly, the UK's coalition government put forward austerity as a time-limited process deigned to restore the country's competitive edge in a global market.

In this sense, it is neatly aligned to the austerity of the Second World War and the promise of better times to come. Crucially, though, there is no external enemy that justifies the logic of the current austerity. The enemy is within – the financial markets of the West – and is not being asked to join in with the frugality of the masses. The notions of collectivity drawn upon with such ease, then, are disingenuous at best, as the difference between private debt and public debt is never explained, merely hidden under a romantic view of the wartime effort, perceived as a happier age of simplicity. As Bramall explains, 'contradictions between "austerity" as it is articulated to anti-consumption and austerity as deficit-reduction have become more striking as the years of recession have persisted'. And, thankfully, the nostalgia of comparing the present to a historical austerity is therefore not ideologically compliant (Bramall, 2013:51). In fact, it becomes increasingly less deniable that cupcake austerity was and is not purely about household economia, but about the vast swath of public cuts that came as part of austerity. Steven Fraser makes exactly this link, arguing that welfare dismantling and individual thrift are intrinsically linked. In making his case he says Americans have already seen the systematic dismantling of public welfare programmes and the 'privatization of collective thrift' during which the burden of risk has been dramatically shifted onto the shoulders of individuals (2011).

Current austerity is, fundamentally, an ideological thrift, tactically used in order to enable the paring back of the welfare state. What is most concerning about this is the way in which it constitutes the widest divide yet witnessed between the logic of personal and public finances; between notions of individual and collective responsibility, yet is presented as a set of social policies that treats the two holistically, and as if one is connected by linear causality to the other. We are, in fact, in an age of illogical thrift, which disavows people of their ability to make social change happen in the realm of everyday life – a reality unconvincingly obscured by rhetoric celebrating the (apparent) light hand of the state.

6

Consumer thrift: Keynes, consumer rights and the new thrifty consumers

The Great Depression, thrift and consumer rights

The previous chapter examined how thrift, as manifested through practices of consuming less, making do, or simply not consuming, was galvanised as a practice to aid the economic, and to some extent ideological, survival of nations. In contrast, this chapter shows how history very quickly came to employ a contrasting logic when it came to promoting action on the part of citizens. It explores an opposite form of thrift – that of being a savvy consumer – and how it was galvanised for much the same ends as making do and mending.

The roots of consumer thrift can be traced back to the US stock-market crash of 1929, which triggered the economic crisis now known as the Great Depression – the most severe and long-lasting depression the United States had ever known. As Jason Smith describes, 'people of all backgrounds had to cope with the utter collapse of the economic system, a collapse so extensive that it exposed the failure of government, business, and society to control the market' (Smith, 2014:1). The depression continued throughout the 1930s, with devastating impacts in both the United States and abroad, especially Europe, where many countries were still recovering from the First World War. In the United States, at the depth of the depression in the early 1930s, one-third of the working population were unemployed, resulting in widespread hunger and homelessness (Watkins, 2010). As Smith says, during the Great Depression 'authorities estimated that between four hundred thousand and two million Americans became transients, people who simply drifted from place to place, wandering across the nation in search of opportunity' (2014:18). People rooted in garbage dumps for food and everywhere enormous queues formed outside soup kitchens.

In the context of the Great Depression, concerns over the rights of consumers had begun to find powerful form in the creation of various consumer organisations. These organisations were informed by an unlikely array of experts and activists who set up the initial consumer movement in the United States based on causes as un-aligned as engineering standards, home economics, calls for improved food and drug laws, the cooperative movement, the labour movement, fledgling consumer organisations and leftist politics. In 1929 democratic and educational theorist John Dewey and progressive economist Paul Douglas founded a new third party, the League for Independent Political Action, around the interests of consumers, saying 'the needs and troubles of the people are connected with problems of consumption, with problems of the maintenance of a reasonably decent and secure standard of living'. They felt the other parties were clinging to production, when the era of industrial expansion had long since passed (Cohen, 2003:27). Meanwhile the consumer movement was inspired by intellectual debate rising out of the thinking of rather unlikely bedfellows President Herbert Hoover, the sci-fi writer Edward Bellamy and the sociologist Thorstein Veblen (see Mayer, 1989).[1]

Hoover, a Republican, promoted partnerships between government and business under the rubric of 'economic modernisation', believed strongly in the Efficiency Movement, which attempted to rationalise the 'wasteful' practices of the government and the economy, and emphasised the importance of volunteerism and of the role of individuals in society and the economy. In contrast, Bellamy was seen as a Marxist sci-fi writer, and indeed his major work – *Looking Backwards* (1888) – features a socialist utopia in which private property was nationalised, an 'industrial army' organised production and distribution, and all citizens are given 'credit cards' with an equal amount of money on them. The book was the third-largest bestseller of its time (after *Uncle Tom's Cabin* and *Ben-Hur: A Tale of the Christ*) and upon its publication immediately inspired a political mass movement in which 'Bellamy Clubs' were set up to discuss and put into action the book's ideas. Thorstein Veblen's *Theory of the Leisure Class* (1899), whilst broadly aligned to Marxist thought in some ways, was in others a treatise in favour of individualism in that he saw conspicuous consumption as un-American because it encouraged the working and middle classes to copy the style of the upper classes rather than seek their own social status, prestige and happiness. Yet the combination of these three somehow gained coherence under the consumer movement.

Even the character generally agreed to have triggered and then led the consumer movement – Frederick Schlink – is intriguing. Schlink wrote *Your Money's Worth* (1927) with Stuart Chase – a book seen as the founding moment of the movement. It was a warning about sales pressure and misleading advertising and saw the creation of consumers clubs nationwide. Schlink then co-authored with Arthur Kallet *One Hundred Million Guinea Pigs* (1933), a book whose title referred to the approximate population of the United States at the time, warning of the lack of safety testing on many common everyday products. However, having founded consumer research, Schlink then refused his workers higher wages and terminated their employment when they went on strike. His focus had been on capitalistic advertising all along, rather than workers' rights, and his actions caused an exodus of employees who set up their own organisation – the Consumers Union. The latter's publication soon surpassed Schlink's, and in its current conception – *Consumer Reports* – it is the leading North American consumer magazine.

This unfathomable range of influences, then, saw a consumer movement in the United States that was seen as coming from the political Left (in fact McCarthy even accused it of harbouring communists), but through which thrift had become about being a wise consumer in light of collective interests instilled by the New Deal, a Democrat-inspired and yet highly commercial plan more aligned to what would be seen as Right-wing policies in the UK.

The New Deal: consuming for national economic recovery

It was also against the backdrop of the Great Depression that the presidential election of 1932 took place, in which the Republican incumbent Herbert Hoover was defeated in a landslide by the Democrat Franklin D. Roosevelt. Once in power, Roosevelt wasted no time in setting in motion a profusion of policies that together constituted the 'New Deal' – programmes designed to bring poverty relief, economic recovery and longer-term political reform. Whereas Hoover had always strongly advanced an argument for limited government and shown a deep respect for the capacity for Americans to help themselves, Roosevelt, in light of the crisis, saw a strong hand of the state as the best, and only, option. He quickly drew around him a group of advisers of like mind who became known as the 'Brains Trust' (see figure 6.1). They were a group of academic experts, recruited by New York politico Samuel Rosenman, all of whom rejected Hoover's philosophical approach. Initially, they consisted of political scientist Raymond Moley, agricultural economist Rexford Tugwell, financial regulation expert Adolf Berle and Roosevelt's former law partner Basil O'Connor. Moley, Tugwell and Berle had their differences, but all three were historical institutionalists who believed that markets were inherently imperfect and that poorly constructed institutions and regulations could severely hurt the economy. In other words, they believed in the necessity of the strong hand of the state.

6.1 Members of the Brains Trust pictured with Roosevelt in 1932

The New Deal programmes were set into action by the passing of the National Industrial Recovery Act (NIRA) in 1933. They were primarily concerned with administering resources, seeking to re-establish foreign markets that could soak up US surplus production, addressing the issue of under-consumption on the part of US citizens, and of distributing wealth and products more equitably. As Smith argues, the NIRA is best thought of as the public policy cornerstone of the New Deal's early years from 1933 to 1935 (Smith, 2014:45). Smith describes Title 1 of the NIRA as a 'virtual declaration of war on the Depression', whilst Title II expanded and formalised the New Deal's public works policy (2014:45). In its all-out assault, Title I set out a series of goals for business and labour, which required workers and firms to collaborate in setting prices, wages, hours and production goals. The idea was that in so doing, they would be able to stimulate both consumption and production of agricultural and industrial products. To accomplish this, Roosevelt created the National Recovery Administration (NRA) and gave it the responsibility of carrying out Title I of the NIRA. It is worth noting that other nations also suffering as a result of the Great Depression used the new deal as a kind of blueprint for their own revivals. In France, the Popular Front government of Léon Blum was called the 'The French New Deal'; in Belgium the national unity government of Paul Van Zeeland was seen as pursuing a copy of the American New Deal; and in Britain David Lloyd George called for a 'New Deal' for Great Britain.

Well-aware of the potential for the radical nature of these programmes to cause a backlash, Roosevelt took the unusual and inspired decision to limit the influence of the press by broadcasting regular 'fireside chats' on the radio, in which he explained warmly and in simple language the latest moves of the New Deal. They were extremely popular across the United States and succeeded in maintaining calm and uniting the populace behind him. They also served, albeit probably unintentionally, to disguise the fact that in a broader sense, the New Deal was not simply about programmes and resources and allocation, it was also about instilling new economic attitudes in the American populace. The New Deal saw the power of the federal government expanded and deployed in order to address the dramatic failures of the market economy. As Smith argues, the New Deal's reforms did not only manage to halt the depression (although not end the crisis), but they 'profoundly changed the American economy, society, and political system in ways that still resonate today' (Smith, 2014:2). It was not simply a set of economic reforms aimed at saving the nation, but also a political project specific to the Democratic Party at the time. Roosevelt declared that the federal government needed to develop 'an economic declaration of rights' in order to safeguard the rights of individuals to make a comfortable living.

What the New Deal taught the American people was that not only was the thrift of the depression no longer necessary, but it would actually harm recovery. Being thrifty was now about consuming wisely and well; the consumer, not just the worker, was now all-important for the economic survival of a nation. So, contrary to conservative interpretations, it was far from anti-capitalist; rather, it created a new version of capitalism – one in which thrift was most definitely the enemy. As Smith maintains, 'the New Dealers certainly brought about dramatic changes, but they were not radicals who were deeply opposed to capitalism or the vitality of the market economy. Rather … they were reformers who were deeply interested in fixing the problems of capitalism' (2014:2).

The emphasis on consumption, and on the ability of citizens to be able to show their prowess in thrifty consumption, brought with it a new set of debates around who could consume. The 'negro shopper' was suddenly welcome in stores across the United States as best exemplified by the 1954 film *The Secret of Selling to the Negro*.[2] This rise in conspicuous consumption amongst African-Americans saw sociologist E. Franklin Frazier write *Black Bourgeoisie*, about a new African-American elite who indulged in conspicuous consumption in their own black worlds. For Frazier the old black middle class had evolved from one [and proximity to white culture?] in which genteel manners, folk traditions and religious practices were central, to one with a more secular outlook which measured its own success by occupational status and income level. However, according to Frazier this new class lacked a firm place in the American economy and whilst they looked down upon lower black classes, often disassociating themselves from their African roots and slave pasts, they were rejected by white Americans causing them to feel inferior. To compensate they engaged in mythmaking about their success, engaging in conspicuous consumption to support such fantasies (2002). All this is of course not dissimilar to Franz Fanon's much later thinking in *Black Skin, White Masks* in which he berated the manners and dress of ex-slaves who attempted to take on what he saw as 'White habits'. He saw this as creating a divided self-perception of amongst 'black subjects' who has lost their native cultural origins by embracing another culture, and believed it to be responsible for producing an inferiority complex in the mind of such subjects, who attempted to imitate the culture of the coloniser (1986).

This new African-American class of conspicuous consumers plays interestingly alongside Patrick Rael's contention that the virtues of thrift were seen as belonging to white people, whilst black people were defined in contrast as lazy, profligate and improvident (2011). Thrift in this context then was seen as a somehow biologically determined characteristic as opposed to a skill required to be mastered by a certain economic class.[3] Rael is specifically commenting on the period from the revolution to the civil war, but it is entirely possible that such attitudes were part of what both the new consumer market's slowness to welcome the black consumer, and the black consumer's apparent determination (following Frazier's argument) to prove themselves reliable and able to manage money as the thrifty yet conspicuous consumers that the New Deal era demanded. In this sense such consumers were going against the earlier twentieth-century ideas of Booker T. Washington, that constitutional rights would be brought about for Black Americans through thrift, hard work, Christian character and the material advancement this would bring.[4]

Certainly, the rise of the African-American shopper brings into question the famous findings of husband and wife team Robert and Helen Lynd, who, in their famous anthropological studies of the fictional city of 'Middletown', found that the generally Republican business class grudgingly accepted the money the New Deal brought in, but immediately returned to their former practices once it was no longer needed because it did not sit well with their Republican outlook (Lynd and Lynd, 1937).[5] Essentially, the Lynds argued that the New Deal changed very little. Whilst this may have been true for the largely white business class in 'Middletown', it was certainly not the case for other demographics.

Keynesian economics and the duty to consume

It is impossible to mention the New Deal without acknowledging the presence of John Maynard Keynes. Whilst valid claims that the link between the two is not as straightforward as historical accounts have often made out, it is undeniable that Keynes' key views certainly resonated and had some impact on Roosevelt and the Brains Trust advisors to him at the time. After all, the crux of Keynes' worldview was economic interventionism, which he deemed necessary to combat the cycles of boom and bust present in any national economy; and economic interventionism was precisely what Roosevelt launched into with the New Deal policies. Key to this was Keynes' rejection of Say's law, which, briefly put, asserts that supply will create its own demand.[6] In other words, increased production will automatically lead to increased consumption – markets will be created as products emerge. In contrast, Keynes believed in the necessity of government investment. (This is best articulated in his *General Theory of Employment, Interest and Money*, 1936.) Hence, Roosevelt's government began to cautiously embrace Keynes, investing in stimulus packages in order to expand consumption, which would soak up the increased production, and in turn lead to higher employment. By the late 1930s, Keynesianism was widely accepted by US government economists (Cohen, 2003: 54) and other countries were beginning to follow suit.

Under this new logic, consumption was effectively keeping people in jobs. Indeed, Keynes was quick to link the negative aspects of unemployment to the insufficiency of the propensity to consume and this idea was central to his theory of effective demand. In particular, Keynesian logic utilised the 'paradox of thrift' to encourage consumption by all for the salvation of the nation. Put briefly, the paradox is that if every individual person saves, demand (consumption) will fall, economic growth will decrease, wages will, therefore, decrease too and the population as a whole will suffer. Therefore, according to the argument, whilst thrift is good on an individual level, it cannot be generalised, as collective thrift would have a negative impact on the economy and therefore on the population as a whole.

As Keynes admitted, Bernard Mandeville had, in fact, picked up on the idea that was to become the paradox of thrift as early as 1714 in his *Fable of the Bees*.

The fable describes a kingdom in which all consumption had been curtailed and as a result the kingdom had failed to survive intact, the remaining bees fleeing the hive, and in it Mandeville advocated allowing the 'private vice' of greed in view of the 'public benefits' it entailed – 'Thus every part was full of vice, Yet the whole mass a paradise' (1997). With these lines, Mandeville effectively outlined what Adam Smith would come to argue seventy years later – that 'consumption is the sole end and purpose of all production and the interest of the producer ought to be attended to, only so far as it may be necessary for promoting that of the consumer' (2003:56). Keynes described the poem as outlining 'the appalling plight of a prosperous community in which all the citizens suddenly take it into their heads to abandon luxurious living, and the State to cut down armaments, in the interests of Saving' (Keynes, 1964:360).

This idea of the wealth of the few somehow enabling a better life for the many is, of course, the basis for 'trickle-down' economics and this marked a fundamental change concerning capitalism's relationship with itself. As previously mentioned, capitalism has proceeded down a line stemming from Augustinian thought in which avarice was seen as able to be commandeered in order to guard against other more detrimental passions (such as lust) – this avarice was what Mandeville talked of when he said that every part was full of 'vice'. This led to the Keynesian idea of benefits for all and the political rhetoric of the duty to consume. However, in travelling this path in which money is posited as capable of doing good, capitalism had also requisitioned a rather more Aristotelian notion of money as 'bad', taking the 'sin of the miser' and transforming it into something more akin to 'the sin of the saver'.

The onset of Keynesian thought meant that thrift began to be penalised throughout Western economies. This was most apparent of course in Keynes' *General Theory of Employment, Interest and Money* (1936), but can also be seen in new Liberal economists J. A. Hobson and A. F. Mummery's *Physiology of Industry* (1889), in which they claimed that saving resulted in the underemployment of capital and labour during trade depressions: 'the East End problem, with its concomitant of vice and misery, is traced to its economic cause … the most respectable and highly extolled virtue of thrift' (1889:88). The liberal economist F. A. Hayek wrote in 1976 that 'it is probably a misfortune that, especially in the USA, popular writers like Samuel Smiles … have defended free enterprise on the ground that it regularly rewards the deserving, and it bodes ill for the future of the market order that this seems to have become the only defense of it which is understood by the general public. That it has largely become the basis of the self-esteem of the businessman often gives him an air of self-righteousness which does not make him more popular' (1982:74). Hayek of course, wanted free enterprise to be defended on the grounds that it played to 'natural' competitive urges and innate and irreducible social Darwinism.

With the Keynesian revolution then, it was suddenly consumers, not producers, who were deemed responsible for higher productivity and full employment. There was, essentially, a *duty* to spend. Not surprisingly, these changes in economic theory and policy caused cultural changes too. Once the thrift of the Second World War was over, there was a notable change across the United States and Western Europe in attitudes towards consumption, and it is often hailed as the 'moment' that consumer society was born. There has been much written about the birth of consumerism – when it happened, what it was and, indeed, whether it occurred at a specific 'moment' at all. The problem seems, in part at least, to be one of a lack of clarity surrounding the terms 'consumption' on the one hand, and 'consumerism' on the other. Whilst there is now little doubt that various countries at various points in history had very active mercantile economies in which consumption was very much part of everyday life, it is less easy to argue that a consumerist culture had therefore become an overwhelming factor. Consumerism in this sense is more frequently described as a twentieth-century phenomenon; one that came hand in hand with the mass consumption of the postwar years. There is no room here for a full discussion of the merits of denying a 'moment' of mass consumption or a consumerist turn as such in the West, suffice it to say that what is interesting and defining about the postwar moment is that for the first time there were 'instructions' from above (i.e. government policies and messages) to spend (see McKendrick *et al.*, 1984, for a discussion of the beginning of consumer society). It was, therefore, however we view the wider history of consumerism, a moment in which people were specifically constructed as consumers and told that being a consumer was part of their national duty. Whilst consumerism may have been rife in other eras, it did not conceive of the individual as an economic unit required to spend for the survival of the nation. It was the economic *necessity* for consumption – the *duty* to spend – that marked the true beginning of consumer society as we now know it.

That said, it was not a 'duty' that was promoted as in any way dull of course. Rather, it was re-branded as a 'freedom'. The consumer as a desiring subject was born, and the idea that one might differentiate oneself from others via the purchase of specific products. Marketing, as an industry, emerged in order to 'inform' the consumer on how these products could enable them to individuate themselves. Consumption, it seemed, was now about self-actualisation, and 'freedom', whereas thrift had apparently necessarily denied people this opportunity. This emphasis on freedom and just how deep into belief systems it went is captured well by Roosevelt's acceptance speech in 1936, in which he stated, 'today we stand committed to the proposition that freedom is no half and half affair. If the average citizen is guaranteed equal opportunity in the polling place, he must have equal opportunity in the market place' (1938). It is not difficult to see the line from Tocqueville, to Roosevelt, to Milton Friedman, in such statements.

Consumption became *consumerism* and the hedonistic consumer was born. Wartime pleas for thrift and making do turned to vociferous encouragements to spend and enjoy in the postwar years, not least as a result of the ways in which both Keynesian logic and the consumer culture of the United States began to feed into everyday British society. This is not to say pleasure-seeking consumption had not existed previously, but it had not been such a mainstream and state-sponsored activity. Nor had 'the consumer' been constructed in quite such conscious ways as became the case following the Second World War. She (and it was predominantly a she that was depicted) had existed, but had not been 'invented' as such. She became part of a normalisation of women as pleasure-seeking materialists, rather than stoic providers of their family's needs. She was transformed from the Mrs Sew-and-Sew of wartime thrift campaigns, fulfilling her family's needs as best she could, to the frivolous Lucy in *I Love Lucy* – a 'liberated', 'modern', carefree to the point of being flippant, and desirous shopper, fulfilling her own desire for pleasure in her new-found leisure-time that modern labour-saving consumer devices, such as washing machines, had provided her with.

Lucy, as an embodiment of this newly constructed female consumer, was, in effect, a vehicle for the evangelists of modernity to promote a world that appeared cleaner, lighter, more efficient and, above all, more fun than previously. The modern device-loving, consumer-housewife was the epitome of the good Keynesian pleasure-seeking shopper, so opposite to the thrift-loving housewife of the war years, and so suddenly changed. Consumption may have provided pleasure before, but this pleasure now *belonged* to the consumer, and she was encouraged to see it as her right. Yet, just as the pre-Keynesian Mrs Sew-and-Sew had a duty, so too did the Keynesian pleasure-seeker. Her duty was to foster her own desire, in order that consumer demand be maintained, and so the economic health of the nation. At one level, the female consumer was still being the Florence Nightingale of the economy, only now her nursing was about spending, not scrimping – consumption, not thrift.

Contemporaneously to (Keynesians would argue as a result of) this new economic logic, pre-war levels of prosperity began to return in the 1950s. The wartime age-of-austerity was over, and by the mid-1950s David Kynaston's 'age of modernity' had arrived (2008). The 1950s and 1960s were in many ways a golden age – at least compared to what had come before. There was a dramatic rise in the average standard of living due largely to a rise in real wages. Coupled with this, unemployment averaged at an incredibly low 2 per cent, making attitudes towards working mothers more relaxed and seeing the onset of the two-income family. This meant that disposable income was at an all-time high and consumer spending increased dramatically – a phenomenon heightened by the loosening of credit controls. In fact, by the early 1960s the majority of Britons enjoyed a level of prosperity that had previously been known only to a small minority of the population. Small local stores were replaced by large chain stores and shopping centres, and cars became a significant part of British life. According to John Burnett, by 1963, 30 per cent of all private households had a refrigerator, 45 per cent a washing machine, 72 per cent a vacuum cleaner, and, most telling of all, 82 per cent had a television (1986:302).

In reality of course, this 'freedom' may not always have felt very 'free'. As Yates and Hunter argue, by 1950 classic thrift had gradually been displaced by a consumer thrift that was counter-intuitive to both Puritan and classic thrift as it focused on buying consumer goods 'on time'. In other words, credit emerged as thrift related to time and it was at this point that work began to have to always be catching up with money already spent. (Not surprisingly, thrift in the sense of thriving often attempts the opposite of this – to re-gain time and quality of life by not needing to earn as much by dint of practising economic frugality!) As a result of this, there was a far greater reliance upon income, credit and time than anyone cared to admit. The apparent beauty of Keynesianism was the way in which it relied upon spending as opposed to hard work and thrift. However, it soon became clear for many people that greater levels of income were required for spending to take place, and that for many this required borrowing at high levels of interest followed by debt that was difficult to pay off and trapped workers in often unsuitable employment conditions. Whereas previous versions of thrift had focused on saving for potential future need, this new consumer thrift was explicitly concerned with saving in order to be able to continue spending (even if in small amounts) in the present. It was about making savings on consumer goods, as opposed to saving (i.e. not spending) money – hence the growing acceptability at the time of credit facilities.

In addition, this model of rising consumption was associated with longer working hours, as Richard Titmuss had argued earlier, to explain the apparent rise of the 'Affluent Society' in the late 1950s (Titmuss, 1962) and captured more recently in the concept of 'time poverty' (de Graaf, 2003). In addition, of course, the postwar generation of so-called 'baby-boomers', having paid off their mortgages, had surplus income with which to become further indebted, or to pass on to their children. This interpretation is also consistent with a Regulation Theory approach, which helped to explain the ability of capitalism to stabilise itself in the 1970s and 1980s, but might also help explain the illusion of 'stability' during the long boom of the last decade (Boyer, 1990; Aglietta, 1997; Jessop and Sum, 2006). The model of growth at the dawn of the twenty-first century was one of enhanced personal consumption on the basis of negotiated debt.

The citizen-consumer

When Roosevelt had spoken about consuming and voting as equally important freedoms, he had perhaps not realised quite how accurate a portrayal this was of the citizens that would emerge from the postwar era. It is no exaggeration to say that the creation of thrifty, well-informed consumption as a personal and individual duty (especially a national duty), led to a new kind of citizen, not only in the United States, but in other countries where what might be called a general mentality of Keynesian logic had come into play. As Lizabeth Cohen argues, despite the ways in which Americans' identities as citizens and consumers have often been presented as opposites – as citizens embracing a larger public interest, and as consumers concerned with private material desires – over the course of the twentieth century, they have become impossible to separate (2003:8). According to Cohen, in the postwar 'Consumers Republic' a new ideal emerged – the purchaser as citizen – a consumer who, in satisfying personal material wants, actually served the national interest (2003:9).

Cohen also argues that, more recently, a new combined 'consumer/citizen, taxpayer, voter' has emerged, and gained influence in a 'Consumerized Republic' (2003:9). In this latter Republic, self-interested citizens view government policies as they would other market transactions, judging them by how well they serve them personally (2003:9). The duty of the citizen-consumer is purportedly one that helps the whole of society, but its fulfilment by consumers is one that based on their own individual agendas. Certainly, the embedding of the cultural attitude towards consumption (and therefore thrift) following the New Deal fundamentally changed the relationship between the individual consumer, the market and the state. As it was now important to be a good consumer for the sake of your country's economy, one became a citizen-consumer, with a national and civic duty to consume. During the New Deal the National Recovery Association (NRA) ran patriotic campaigns with made up slogans encouraging people to spend. These frequently placed consumer protection a very obvious second to the apparently mutual interests of business and consumers, for example the 'blue eagle' display cards that read 'When you buy cigars you help provide incomes for farmers, labor, salesmen, dealers and yourself. Buy now'.

As Cohen points out, the NRA functioned within a classical economic paradigm, in which recovery was seen as depending upon efficient production triggering increased consumption – rather than demand for products and higher consumption triggering higher levels of production – or 'Say's Law' (2003:28). Consumer-minded economists and reformers overcame Say's Law by arguing that the economy was basically founded on consumption, not production. As a result, consumerism began to be seen not just as stimulating a stagnant economy, but as enabling unprecedented growth. It became the answer in both Britain and the United States, and in fact, previous attitudes towards thrift became despised, particularly in the United States, as part of a kind of miserable puritanism, preachy and pointless. For example, in *The Magnificent Ambersons* (1918), Booth Tarkington explains how the theatre in town did not do well financially because the people were too thrifty due to being 'the sons or grandsons of the early settlers, who had opened the wilderness ... with wagons and axes and guns, but with no money at all. The pioneers were thrifty or they would have perished ... they left traces of that fear in their sons and grandsons ... No matter how prosperous they were, they could not spend money either upon art, or upon mere luxury and entertainment, without a sense of sin'. These changes in the perceived role of the consumer, both on the part of consumers themselves, but also on the part of governmental and market actors, are well captured by Frank Mort in his thought-provoking summary. As he argues, 'the citizen subjects of democratic politics and the subjects of commercially driven consumer culture were understood to be intimately connected' (2006:226).

7

Ecological thrift: frugality, de-growth and Voluntary Simplicity

Thrift as a tool for de-growth

Discourses around frugality and the environment are by no means new, and voices from across academic disciplines call for thrift from a broadly ecological standpoint, and have done for many decades. Several well-researched and bestselling reports on the threatened state of the global environment saw public awareness grow from the 1970s onwards. Key amongst these was Rachel Carson's *Silent Spring* (1962) and the Club of Rome's *Limits to Growth* report (1972). The first Earth Day, celebrated on 21 March 1970, marked the emergence of an environmental movement in the United States that reasserted the need for a frugality ethos in order to protect the planet from pollution and other afflictions (Fritsch, 1974). All these essentially introduced the concept of gradual but profound environmental destruction by industry.

By 1983, the United Nations had established the World Commission on Environment and Development (WCED), better known as the Brundtland commission after its chairwoman, Gro Harlem Brundtland. The Brundtland report that arose from the commission defined sustainable development as meeting 'the needs of the present without compromising the ability of future generations to meet their own needs'. This phrase was widely endorsed and has remained the most widely accepted starting point for scholars and practitioners, despite many arguing that development (understood as industrialising and capitalistic) is simply incompatible with sustainability. The report did however make important contributions in not only raising awareness, but also by insisting that it was no longer population growth (in the developing world) that was the major threat to the environment, but the use of fossil fuels by those in the developed world. This put the emphasis for change on the West and its habits and was a sizeable shift from previous thinking. Summits such as the 1992 Earth Summit in Rio further pushed the idea of sustainable development.

Furthermore, consumption (and non-consumption) specifically features in the logic of these debates. For example, Agenda 21, the policy document that arose from the Rio Earth Summit in 1992, drew attention to the environmental impacts of consumption, which were identified as the major cause of environmental degradation (UNDP, 1998; OECD, 2002). Similarly, the 2002 World Summit on Sustainable Development identified changing patterns of consumption as one of its three main objectives. So, despite going through periods of being deeply unfashionable, discourses on frugality when in connection with environmental issues such as those recognised throughout the history above, have never really retired altogether. In 1995, James Nash, a Christian ethicist, wrote an article discussing the decline of the virtue of frugality. In it, he stated, 'not only is frugality demoted by our society, but it is also met with ridicule and depicted as unfashionable, unpalatable, and even unpatriotic'. Nash argued that contrary to this ridicule, frugality ought to be perceived as an 'earth affirming and enriching norm that delights in the non- and less-consumptive joys of the mind and flesh, especially the enhanced lives for human communities and other creatures that only constrained consumption and production can make possible on a finite planet'. For Nash frugality was most definitely not a 'world-denying asceticism', or 'the triumph of the spirit over the flesh', although he did acknowledge that frugal people could, however, only flourish and function effectively within societies committed to being frugal and which had created regulations and an ethos that would support it (1995:33). The article became a seminal one, proving that it is far harder to hate the morality of thrift as frugality when it is for the sake of the planet.

None of these concerns are new; they are simply acknowledged as more pressing in the current day. In many ways the ecological imperative has enabled a discourse around frugality that is less 'moral' in a limited Marxist way than it used to be, and more 'ethical' in terms of finding ways to live differently for quite practical reasons. Most recently, these concerns have been crystalised in the increasingly mainstream term – Anthropocene. The term, coined by ecologist Eugene Stoermer and atmospheric chemist Paul Crutzen, describes the current geological era, positing it as a massive increase in human influence on the world during the last 150 years and especially since 1950. Embedded in the concept is the idea that the Anthropocene represents a fundamental break with past experience – that humankind's effect has become so dominant as to be best understood as a new era/new way of being on earth.

Despite bringing ecological imperatives to the fore, many commentators feel the idea of the Anthropocene comes with its own issues. For example, many mainstream positive discourses tend to suggest that technology will enable us to address climate change and save ourselves from destruction without any major reform of economic or political systems. In such discourses the central motif of reconciling the tensions between technology and ecology, economic growth and ecology, and competitive market and ecology becomes one of the correct employment of smart technology and 'win-win strategies' (Milne et al., 2006). Such suggestions however, have come with severe criticisms, particularly from those who argue it is precisely economic growth that needs to be called into question (see Trainer, 2000; Carruthers, 2001; de Geus, 2003; Milne et al., 2006; Scott-Cato, 2006). In addition, many commentators feel the term does not sufficiently recognise the role of capitalism in environmental destruction, or that it is capitalism rather than environmental practice that needs to change (see Malm, 2016; Sklair, 2016).

Much, but not all, of this critique of neo-classical economics and its assumptions of the necessity of growth are explicitly anti-capitalist. Here, Andreas Malm's work on 'fossil capital' is key. Malm argued that the shift to steam power took place essentially because it allowed capitalists to better exploit labour by giving them better access to and control over workers, as coal could be moved around, enabling the capitalist to take the power to the people, rather than having to take the people to the power (2016:17). For Malm, steam was essentially used as a form of power by the newly rising capitalist class against industrial workers. Whilst Malm's study is based on the rise of capitalism in Britain, he makes the point that the shifts involved did not remain confined to Britain; in fact the fossil fuel economy quickly spread to many other parts of the globe. Thus, whilst climate change will affect us all, it can be seen as having been brought on by a specific group of capitalists whose class interests lay in the adoption of fossil fuels. In a related argument, in *Facing the Anthropocene*, Ian Angus forcefully argues that capitalism's inexorable drive for growth, powered by the rapid burning of fossil fuels that took millions of years to form, has driven the planet to the brink of disaster, and that survival will require nothing short of radical social change in which fossil capitalism is replaced with a new, 'ecosocialist' civilisation (2016).

Radical questioning of economic growth has led to the concept of de-growth. As a concept, it originates from the work of thinkers including Marx (1859), Jevons (1865), Soddy (1922, 1926), Polanyi (1944), Illich (1973, 1977), Schumacher (1973) and Hirsch (1976). Essentially it can be defined as a new economic paradigm based on the scientific idea of entropy. Indeed, the term *décroissance* (de-growth) first appeared in the French translation of Georgescu-Roegen's (1971) seminal work *The Entropy Law and the Economic Process*. Since then it has been brought to the fore by various writers initially centred in France, but namely Latouche, Aries, Cheney and Schneider. As Latouche points out, though, decroissance is a term that has only been employed since around 2006, despite the fact that related terms such as zero growth, sustainable development and steady state have been relatively commonplace for a few decades (2010a:519). As Latouche says, it is about abandoning the idea of growth for the sake of growth which sees an 'unrestrained search for profit by the holders of capital' and is disastrous for the environment (2010a:519). André Gorz wrote, 'even at zero growth, the continued consumption of scarce resources will inevitably result in exhausting them completely. The point is not to refrain from consuming more and more, but to consume less and less – there is no other way of conserving the available reserves for future generations' (1975:13). More recently, environmental scientist Giorgos Kallis has become a leading force in the burgeoning research network centred in Barcelona, and has focused on using de-growth as a 'missile word', slogan, theory, literature, critique, policy, movement, way of life and attack on the ideology of economic growth (2015).

Based on the accumulated work of the thinkers mentioned above, de-growth is a radical critique of neo-classical thinking on economic growth. As Andreonia and Galmarini say, the de-growth paradigm 'proposes a solution that consists of reducing the scale of the socio-economic system to fit within the biophysical limits of the planet' (2013:65). Perhaps most importantly, de-growth insists upon the incompatibility of consumer capitalism and ecological sustainability. As Fournier attests, 'proponents of de-growth seek to challenge the "naturalness", the supposed inevitability and desirability of growth; they oppose the ideology of growth (more than growth in itself which is no more than an arbitrary calculation)' (2008:532). As Demaria and Kothari argue, 'de-growth calls for a rejection of the obsession with economic growth as a panacea for the solution of all problems. It should not be interpreted in its literal meaning (decrease of the gross domestic product) because that phenomenon already has a name: it is called recession. De-growth does not mean "less of the same"; it is simply different' (2017:2594). This stance is perhaps most famously borne out by Tim Jackson's classic book *Prosperity without Growth*, which fiercely challenged conventional economics and openly questioned the continued pursuit of exponential economic growth. It attempts to demonstrate just how precise, definable and essentially achievable a task building a post-growth economy would be, focusing on the nature of enterprise, the quality of our working lives and the structure of investment amongst other factors (Jackson, 2016).

Similarly, as Schneider *et al.* are keen to point out, de-growth is not equivalent to economic recession or depression – that is, unplanned and involuntary economic de-growth within a growth-driven system, with all the negative consequences it entails (2011). Rather, it is an intentional process involving what Odum and Odum describe as a smooth and prosperous 'way down' (2001). However, this ideology is absolutely not about a return to pre-industrial times. As Schneider et al. assert, it is about introducing innovations to consume and produce less (frugal innovation, innovations that integrate the existence of limits), instead of innovations dedicated to suppressing limits to growth, which leads to rebound (2011). In fact, the 'smooth and prosperous way down' is best explained by Latouche who insists de-growth is not about replacing 'bad' economy with 'good economy' or 'bad' development with 'good' development, by being green, or social or equitable, but about 'just leaving' the economy. In much the same way, Valerie Fournier argues, 'it is not sufficient to call for lesser, slower or greener growth for this would leave us trapped within the same economic logic; rather we need to escape from the economy as a system of representation. This means re-imagining economic relations, identities, activities in different terms' (2008:529).

Similarly, Sklair says the solution to the ecological imperative does not lie in challenging the market, but in ignoring it (2016:109). For him the only solution is post-capitalist, and lies in the creation of small-scale autonomous communities of solidarity based on networks of relatively small producer-consumer cooperatives cooperating at a variety of levels to accomplish a variety of societal tasks. Sklair gives the example of Marcin Jakubowski (a physics PhD disillusioned with academia) who in 2003 created Open Source Ecology (OSE). OSE is a network of farmers, engineers, architects and supporters, whose main goal is the eventual manufacturing of the Global Village Construction Set (GVCS). As described by OSE, 'the GVCS is an open technological platform that allows for the easy fabrication of the 50 different Industrial Machines that it takes to build a small civilization with modern comforts' (Jakubowski, 2011; see figure 7.1). Though it is very early days, it is worth speculating that – give or take a few more or less machines – the GVCS might provide some clues about the size and scope of the optimum producer–consumer cooperative (P-CC) or local network of P-CCs. Whilst it is unclear what the political agenda of OSE is (or, indeed, if they have one that goes beyond producing basic machines that are much cheaper than their corporate counterparts), this type of initiative is invaluable for all those who wish to escape the domination of the market and the state whilst retaining (and, hopefully) improving scientific and technological advances (Sklair, 2016:107–108).

It is these small-scale societies, Sklair argues, that are 'the only way for us to re-connect with nature, to create communities where everyone is responsible to a greater or lesser degree for all the necessities of life and a decent standard of living. To accomplish this, we need to move beyond hierarchy and the state and create

Ecological thrift 97

The Global Village Construction Set

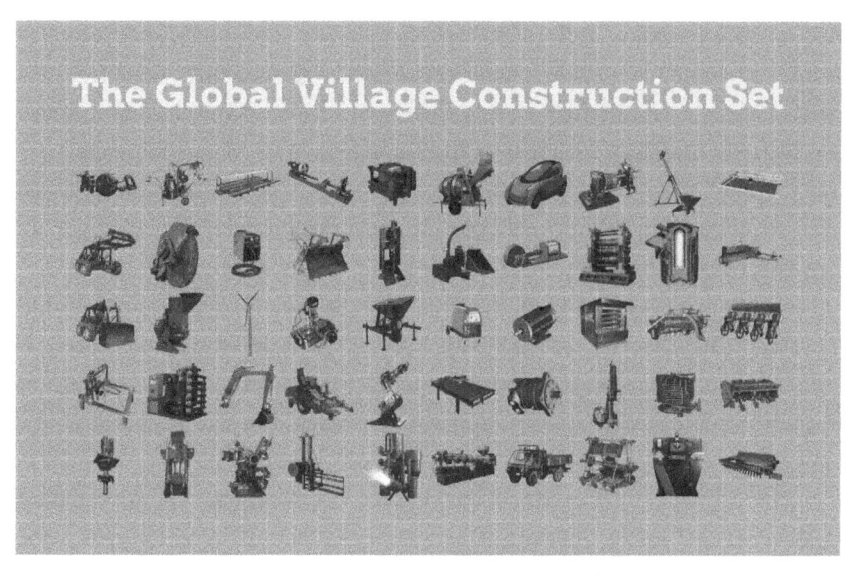

[image of fifty machine icons arranged in a grid]

7.1 The Global Village Construction Set: the fifty machines needed to build a small civilisation

forms of non-capitalist, non-exploitative, alternative globalizations' (2016:106). This is explicitly about decolonising 'the imaginary of growth (continuous economic growth as the ultimate good) and establish de-growth as the common-sense conception of a sustainable and convivial future' (2016:108). Sklair's vision here is not dissimilar to Illich's classic vision of 'modern subsistence' which he defines as 'the lifestyle in a post-industrial economy within which people succeed in reducing their dependence on the market, and reach that point whilst protecting – by political means – an infrastructure in which technology and tools are useful first and foremost to create practical values' (Illich, 1977:87–88).

Interestingly, Latouche makes the argument that the economy is a religion, saying 'when we say that … one should speak about a-growth the same way that one speaks about atheism, it means precisely that; to become atheists of growth and the economy' (2010a:521). This is particularly interesting in historical context. Worship of the economy now can usefully be compared to worship of God in previous eras. In both cases the object of worship is seen as an all-powerful external being, and is spoken about as if it is not made up of the citizens of the planet. Thus, religious thrift is replaced with religio-economic thrift, and in both cases the God-like element is what takes the thriving out of thrift. (Perhaps it is no coincidence that religious groups who did not see God as external and all-powerful, but rather within humans, such as the Quakers, held a version of thrift that was far closer to thriving than frugality.) In fact, perhaps there is something about not feeling in control to be said here; a sense that if citizens are at the behest of an all-powerful external being then thriving is not in their own hands, and all that can be done is to be frugal and hope for the best. In contrast, once the idea of power being in another entity's hands is removed, then thriving becomes more important and more *possible* – humankind can make decisions to thrive because they are not waiting for either God or the economy to enable the good times.

Indeed, the creation of enjoyable lives through our own autonomous human endeavours has become an important part of the de-growth discourse. In addition to arguing for a quantitative reduction in production and consumption, de-growth places emphasis on human well-being through reciprocity and conviviality (see Bonaiuti, 2001, 2005; Georgescu-Roegen, 2004; Ariès, 2005, Latouche, 2005, 2010). This idea of conviviality originates with the work of Illich who describes it as 'the opposite of industrial productivity … autonomous and creative intercourse among persons, and the intercourse of persons with their environment' (1973:11). He argues, 'people need not only to obtain things, they need above all the freedom to make things among which they can live, to give shape to them according to their own tastes, and to put them to use in caring for and about others' (1973:11).

More recently conviviality has been aligned with the idea of reciprocity. As Andreonia and Galmarini argue, 'the concept of de-growth leads to a radical criticism of the neoclassical approach of economic growth and proposes an alternative socio-economic paradigm based on the concept of "reciprocity work"' (2013:64). 'Reciprocity work' can be defined as 'labour devoted to society without monetary compensation but with compensation in terms of goods and services provided in a system of reciprocity', and exists as a mix of social work, unpaid activities, self-production and cooperation among individuals (Andreonia and Galmarini, 2013:68). It is linked to conviviality in that it is assumed to be able to increase social capital by promoting mutual sustainability, community support and social relationships – all aspects of conviviality, itself defined as non-market relationships aimed at improving cooperation and social relationships (Andreonia and Galmarini, 2013:68). Andreonia and Galmarini cite both co-housing and the Voluntary Simplicity movement as examples of conviviality. Examples of communities attempting such reciprocal and convivial models include buen vivir (Latin America), Ecological Swaraj and Radical Ecological Democracy (India), Ubuntu (South Africa) and Gross National Happiness (Bhutan). We might also include Syriza and Podemos as examples to potentially draw upon.

Many empirical studies have been carried out to explore the potential link between de-growth and well-being, almost all of them concluding that living in a scaled-down way improves human happiness (see for example, Cattaneo *et al.*, 2011; Masferrer-Dodas *et al.*, 2011). Alongside this, many articles compare Western visions for reciprocal and convivial living with non-Western thinking. For example, Damien Roiland insists frugality is not necessarily related to consumption as has been understood since the Enlightenment, but might be better expressed by the Indian terms Jugaad or Gandhian – ways of 'thinking and creating new projects that lead to fruitful solutions for the majority' (2016:571).

De-growth then, is very much concerned with thrift as thriving. It is not simply an economic alternative, but a system of living that challenges the very basis for Smith's economic man. As Susan Paulson most persuasively argues, whilst growth tends to be portrayed as apolitical and impartial, with modern markets appearing 'as timeless mechanisms through which all humans freely organize livelihoods and establish value', de-growth is frequently denounced as an 'ideologically driven imposition that would force unwilling victims to sacrifice their God-given freedoms and to betray innate self-interests' (2017:440). In contrast, argues Paulson, markets are anything but this – 'the commodification of labor and nature, together with the colonization of human habits and worldviews by market-relations and money-value, are historical exceptions brutally imposed in eighteenth and nineteenth century England by efforts to mold human nature for industrial growth' (2017:440). Here she draws upon both Polanyi (1944) and the more recent work of David Harvey (2007), insisting that there is a 'stubborn blindness' to these historical facts is that insists upon certain aspects of human life as 'natural instincts'. Amongst such myths, that of the innately rational Homo economicus maximising utility for individual gain is one that will not go away. In contrast, Paulson asks, 'if Homo sapiens is hard wired for growth, why did per capita ecological footprints increase so late in the game? And so unevenly across human populations?' (2017:441). The question as to why reciprocal man cannot be posited as an equally, if not more, viable model for human behaviour both historically and in the future, will be further discussed in the conclusion.

De-growth and post-development

The concept of post-development can be traced to the certain key texts, including Wolfgang Sachs' *Development Dictionary* (2009), Arturo Escobar's *Encountering Development* (1995), Gilbert Rist's *History of Development* (2014) and most recently Majid Rahnema and Victoria Bawtree's *Post-Development Reader* (1997). As Demaria and Kothari make clear, post-development is about escaping 'a set of policies, instruments and indicators to exit "underdevelopment" and reach that desired condition of "development"' (2017:2593). They make the point that many decades after the notion of development has been understood across the world, only a very few nations are considered 'developed', whilst others struggle to emulate their trajectories and conditions at enormous ecological and social cost to themselves (2017:2593). Post-development theory argues that it is not the lack of implementation of development strategies that is the problem, but the idea of development as 'linear, unidirectional material and financial growth' (2017:2593). It is this questioning of growth in the conventional economic sense that aligns post-development with discourses on de-growth.

Moreover, in much the same way as de-growth is suspicious of solving the crisis of the Anthropocene via smart technology, so post-development tends to reject 'sustainable development' policies that simply 'greenwash' unjust and polluting capitalistic practices. In fact, many post-development theorists reject the term sustainable development completely, believing its two facets to be incompatible. Demaria and Kothari critique the 2030 Agenda for Sustainable Development, saying that more recent conferences have reframed the ecological crisis in light of poverty in developing countries, instead of affluence in developed countries, creating a logic that suggests a nation needs to be rich before it can be environmental, and therefore freeing economic growth of its previous environmental stigma. For them this is a 'watering down of the initial debates of 1970s influenced by the Limits to Growth report', and constitutes 'a kind of Green Keynesianism' (2017:2590). They point out that at the UN Conference for Sustainable Development in 2012, the United Nations Environment Programme (UNEP) published a report that failed to address the trade-off between economic growth and environmental conservation, and conceptualised natural capital as a 'critical economic asset' (2017:2591). The report clearly stated, as they attest, that 'the key aim for a transition to a green economy is to enable economic growth and investment whilst increasing environmental quality and social inclusiveness' (2017:2591). In contrast, post-development proposes the same range of alternatives as de-growth proponents tend to, drawing upon buen vivir, de-growth, ecological swaraj, radical feminisms of various kinds, ubuntu, commoning, solidarity economy, food and energy sovereignty amongst other solutions.

As Paulson says, the de-growth movement has become part of what have become known as 'transition discourses' (2017:435). These are inspired by Karl Polanyi's (1944) use of 'the Great Transformation' to characterise the violent upheaval of lifeways and productive systems with the emergence of industrial market economy in eighteenth- to nineteenth-century England. In contrast, 'the Great Transition' describes the historical shift for the twenty-first century that draws upon thinkers and movements such as British economist Kenneth Boulding (1964), the Stockholm Environment Institute (Raskin *et al.*, 2002), Bhutan Prime Minister Jigme Thinley, the New Economics Foundation (Spratt *et al.*, 2009), and founders of the Italian De-growth Association (Bonaiuti, 2014). Arturo Escobar explains transition discourses as taking their point of departure from 'the notion that the contemporary ecological and social crises are inseparable from the model of social life that has become dominant over the past few centuries' (2015:452).

The burgeoning number of articles and publications on de-growth over the past ten years resonates with critiques of growth made in certain areas of post-development studies (see, for example, Meadows *et al.*, 1972; Douthwaite, 1992; Seabrook, 1993; Escobar, 1995; Trainer, 2000; de Riveros, 2001; Curtis, 2003; Scott-Cato, 2006, to mention only a few examples). Latouche too, connects de-growth to post-development, acknowledging the plural nature of the latter and arguing that 'each society, each culture, must leave totalitarian productivism in its own way, and oppose the unidimensional man, homo economus, an identity based on diversity of roots and traditions' (Latouche, 2010:520). Key to the linking of the two, though, is the work of Arturo Escobar, who argues that de-growth and post-development can be seen as belonging to the larger class of 'transition discourses' that call for a significant paradigmatic or civilisational transformation (2015:451). As Escobar puts it, 'both appeal to broad philosophical, cultural, ecological, and economic critiques of capitalism and the market, growth and development. They share some intellectual and social sources (for example, Illich's critique of industrialism and expert institutions; Polanyi's analysis of the dis-imbedding of the economy from social life; sustained attention to economic and ecological crises)' (2015:456).

As Escobar asserts, there is a huge range of transition discourses, all of which take as their point of departure 'the notion that the contemporary ecological and social crises are inseparable from the model of social life that has become dominant over the past few centuries' whether they see this as defined by industrialism, capitalism, modernity, (neo)liberalism, anthropocentrism, rationalism, patriarchalism, secularism or even Judeo-Christian civilisation. A radical transformation of this mode of social life is the united aim (2015:452). Frequently, this is envisaged as an 'ecology of transformation' (Hathaway and Boff, 2009) made up of concerns about ecological justice, biological and cultural diversity, bioregionalism, rootedness in place, participatory democracy and cooperative self-organisation. One of Escobar's key concerns is the lack of dialogue or cohesive interaction between transition discourses from the global North and those from the global South (2015:451). This is not least because movements often associated with de-growth in the global North – such as Voluntary Simplicity – are often seen as irrelevant or are ridiculed in the global South.

The following section will specifically explore Voluntary Simplicity, including the criticisms levelled at it, but to conclude this section it should be noted that in many ways de-growth and post-development as explored above provide examples of ecological thrift that go a long way towards claiming thrift for the political Left. Certainly, thrift (in its frugal sense) is seen as a tool by de-growth movements, and thrift (in its thriving sense) can be seen as part of these movements advocating of conviviality and reciprocity, with the overall sense very definitely being one of aiming for a general condition of thrift as thriving. Perhaps, in the same as de-growth was and is used as a weapon concept, thrift might also need to be weaponised. Certainly, ecological thrift is proving that far from being capitalism's handmaiden, thrift is already a tool for many on the planet in one of the most concerning, but also exciting and genuine, transitions to befall it.

Voluntary Simplicity and ecology

As previously mentioned, the Voluntary Simplicity movement has been turned to as an example of de-growth in action. For example, Alexander and Ussher explain that 'overconsumption in affluent societies is the root or contributing cause of many of the world's most pressing problems, including environmental degradation, global poverty, peak oil and consumer malaise. This suggests that any transition to a sustainable and just society will require those who are overconsuming to move to far more materially "simple" lifestyles' (2012:66). They point out that whilst many economies around the world are improving their ability to produce commodities more cleanly, ecological impact overall is still rising due to the increasing number of commodities being produced and consumed. This is a phenomenon known as the Jevons Paradox, in which the increase in consumption of a good outweighs the efficiency improvements embedded within its production – fuel-efficient cars are a classic example of the Jevons Paradox (see Polimeni et al., 2008). Therefore, so the argument for simplicity goes, that technology and efficiency improvements are not going to solve the ecological crisis, and certainly not unless consumers in developed countries radically cut back on their current high levels of consumption. Indeed, as Alexander and Ussher point out, there is a vast body of literature on ecological and post-growth economics that argues forcefully that the richest nations should immediately give up the pursuit of growth and move towards a 'steady state' economy or even a period of planned contraction in which qualitative rather than quantitative development is the focus (2012:70).

As Witkowski argues, the Voluntary Simplicity movement became a widely disseminated frugality critique throughout the 1990s – 'numerous newspaper and magazine articles, book-length anti-consumption guides, and a modest selection of scholarly analyses instructed readers about the meaning and practice of varying degrees of voluntary simplicity' (2010:249). In the United States anti-consumption activists held national conferences and formed networks of local consciousness-raising groups, called 'simplicity circles'. Members in the United States were estimated to be in the millions, and the movement was also popular in other parts of the developed world, especially the UK and Australia (Witkowski, 2010:249). It is worth noting that the Voluntary Simplicity movement has no criteria or leaders or organisation; its networks are self-formed and elastic. There is however a 'web of simplicity' website that 'members' can use and the *Simple Living Journal* lists simplicity circles that have requested to be listed.

Voluntary Simplicity tends to be seen as about choosing to limit material consumption in order to free one's resources, primarily money and time, to seek satisfaction through nonmaterial aspects of life (see Etzioni, 1998). Meanwhile, Zavestoski says Voluntary Simplicity is both a belief system and a practice that includes cultivating self-reliance and developing one's intellect (2002). Mary Grigsby's description of the Voluntary Simplicity movement is a useful one. She describes it as being 'concerned with environmental degradation, critical of conspicuous consumption and "careerism", and dissatisfied with the quality of life afforded by full participation in mass consumer society' (2004:1). Voluntary Simplifiers then, are concerned with a more fulfilling life, a stronger community and a decrease in environmental damage (2004:1). In fact she goes on to argue that 'the ideas that are being worked on in the voluntary simplicity movement ... draw on the dominant culture, earlier ideas, and cultures of resistance found in the environmental movement' (2004:7). However, she acknowledges that many of these ideas did not originate in the movement and that other interpretations see it as being built on much older ideas. Elgin (1993) links it to ideas in the

United States in the 1960s; and Shi (2007) emphasises ideas from the 1970s and 1980s that he sees as forming the movement.

The term 'voluntary simplicity' was coined by Richard Gregg in the 1920s. He was the first proponent of the movement in its contemporary form, and drew his inspiration from Confucius and Gandhi amongst others (Doherty and Etzioni, 2003). Like Thoreau, Gregg was also a student of Gandhi and is believed to have first used the term in writing, in his 1936 article – 'The Value of Voluntary Simplicity' – for the Indian journal *VisvaBharati Quarterly*. Today, though, the concept of Voluntary Simplicity can most usefully be attributed to Duane Elgin and Arnold Mitchell who revived it in the 1970s. Elgin adopted the term from Gregg's book when writing the book *Voluntary Simplicity: Toward a Way of Life that is Outwardly Simple, Inwardly Rich* (1993), a book that defined Voluntary Simplicity based on the three central tenets of frugal consumption, ecological awareness and personal growth.

Elgin's is seen as the foundational text for simplifiers, but more recently Joe Dominguez and Vicki Robin's *Your Money or Your Life* (1992), and Cecile Andrew's *The Circle of Simplicity: Return to the Good Life* (1997) have also come to be seen as key reading for simplifiers. Both Dominguez and Robin's book, and Andrews' book, draw upon Alan Durning's book *How Much is Enough? The Consumer Society and the Future of the Earth* (1992). All of these texts, though, stop just short of laying the blame for over-worked, spiritually bereft and un-ecologically sound lives at the doorstep of capitalism. Dominguez and Robin are the strongest in their critique of wage labour, but do not blame this specifically on capitalism.

In practice, Voluntary Simplicity takes a wide variety of forms. Etzioni identifies three variations: a moderate form he calls 'downshifting' which simply sees individuals buy less expensive and often functional or less decorated items; 'strong simplifiers' who give up high levels of income and status in order to gain time and reduce stress; and 'holistic simplifiers' who simplify everything in their lives from work to housing to consumption (Etzioni, 1998). For Etzioni, however, Voluntary Simplicity as a practice tends to be about living within consumer capitalism not in opposition to it. Miles too, asserts that 'any movement against that [consumerist] way of life is merely subsumed within the capitalist system as yet another market niche' (1998:45). In their study of voluntary simplifiers, Shaw and Newholm identify 'downshifters' as those who are primarily concerned with improving their own quality of life, rather than living outside of the mainstream, or escaping capitalism somehow. They differentiate however, between these simplifiers and those who form a second group which they call 'ethical simplifiers', and who are fundamentally motivated by concern for the environment and social justice (including economic systems) (Shaw and Newholm, 2002).

In Huneke's nationwide study of US voluntary simplifiers, motivations were found to include dissatisfaction with high-stress lifestyles, and general anti-consumption attitudes, along with the desire to shift to more satisfying ways to spend time.[1] When asked why they began to practice Voluntary Simplicity, nearly a quarter of respondents cited concern for the natural environment. Nineteen per cent said they wanted to shift the ways they were spending their time and energy, 'wanting more time to spend with family and friends, pursuing intrinsically satisfying activities, or simply having more control over how their time was spent' (Huneke, 2005:530).

The range of Voluntary Simplicity practices can be explained by the range of reasons people enter into it. Interestingly, Elgin himself connects Voluntary Simplicity to the Puritans, and also acknowledges it is influenced by Eastern, Quaker and transcendentalist views amongst others. Grigsby analyses the link between Voluntary Simplicity and Puritanism, arguing that voluntary simplifiers often mention Puritans and see their influence, but feel themselves in other ways very unaligned to Puritan goals as they are not attempting to pursue capitalism or practising Voluntary Simplicity in order to please God. In contrast, their aims are to live well for the planet in this life.

Similarly, despite Methodism not having the economic impact that Wesley would probably have hoped, his maxim on thrift – 'earn all you can, save all you can, give all you can' – has been kept alive by various more recent lifestyle movements and can most clearly be seen in the Voluntary Simplicity movement. In their ethnography of voluntary simplifiers in the United States, Walther et al. argue that many define themselves as part of an evangelical Christian movement, but goes on to quote them as talking about 'stewardship' and directly echoing Wesley's maxim, knowingly or not, therefore, promoting his ideas for proper living (2016).

In addition, there is a good amount of evidence to suggest that for many people, Voluntary Simplicity has more collective, ecological motivations, linked to ideas such as de-growth. In chapter two of her book on the movement, Mary Grigsby focuses specifically on ecological ethics and their relation to Voluntary Simplicity. She argues that 'the core ideology and practices advocated by those in the Voluntary Simplicity movement are imbued with an ecological ethic that maintains that all things in the universe exist in interdependent relationship to one another and that human beings are damaging the sustainability of a continued harmonious cycle of these interdependent relationships through relentless consumption of the earth's resources' (2004:30). Dominguez and Robin say 'all of life is one creation'; Elgin too paints a bleak picture of what will happen if we continue to plunder planet earth, asserting 'ecological ways of living will provide an essential foundation for building post-industrial civilizations' (1993:163–164). So, the link between Voluntary Simplicity and ecology is a well-trodden path.

More concretely, Samuel Alexander and Simon Ussher carried out a fifty-question survey with 2,268 participants from across the world (but primarily from the developed regions of the world), which sought to explore the specific ways in which people were living simply.[2] They found that arguments for simpler living tended to be based on environmental, humanitarian, population, limits to economic growth and peak oil concerns, and were only supported by an argument based on increased happiness. This contradicts Grigsby's view, that despite the movement having ecological concerns, participants tend to focus on the individual as the primary mechanism for change, rather than policy. As Alexander and Ussher argue, this 'characterizes the Simplicity Movement as a movement of people who are seeking to "escape" the system at a personal level, rather than "transform" it at a collective level' (2012:81). In contrast, their results showed that 68 per cent of participants conceived of themselves as part of a movement. This, they argue, means the Voluntary Simplicity movement has acquired the group consciousness necessary in order for it to act collectively for a social or political purpose, rather than simply as isolated and unrelated individuals (2012:81).

The key challenge in Voluntary Simplicity becoming a collective force for change, however, is the aspect of privilege in the movement. Members of course have to have experienced enough in order to voluntarily simplify! Even its own members acknowledge this. As a result, the movement is overwhelmingly white and middle-class. Both Elgin and Mitchell's (1977) and Linda Pierce's (1996–1998) studies found simplifiers to be almost entirely Caucasian, female, highly educated, living in urban or suburban areas, and in their thirties or above with no children living at home. In the Pierce study, 64 per cent were married but 61 per cent had no children living at home. As Schor points out, it is also the case that many voluntary simplifiers have the option of moving back into their middle-class mainstream jobs if they want to, and that many of them are older without children, or whose children have grown up, so they have fewer financial responsibilities (Schor, 1998). As Witkowski argues, simplifiers have tended to be in the middle quintile in terms of household income, and are much more educated than the average American. Therefore, 'unlike the working poor, who are saddled with involuntary simplicity, simplifiers have had enough control over their economic lives to rearrange work schedules or, if need be, change jobs. For many of its proponents, Voluntary Simplicity has had as much to do with the time pressures and pace of life dictated by a highly competitive and marketised economy as it has with overconsumption of material things' (Witkowski, 2010:251).

Similarly, Tom Vanderbilt argues that Voluntary Simplicity is simply a luxury afforded the affluent (1996). Certainly, unless one can find a situation without mortgage or rent, one can only earn less, if one already earns more than one needs – growing one's own food and making one's own clothes would have minimal impact for someone on the minimum wage. The majority of voluntary simplifiers have access to resources such as wealth, education and unique skills that could be traded for high income. In other words, it could be argued that it is far easier for those with cultural capital to become voluntary simplifiers. Grigsby does concede (usefully) that the Voluntary Simplicity movement essentially comes from a place of privilege, saying that members 'don't fully acknowledge their own embeddedness in institutionalized patterns of power … The stress, clutter, health problems, lack of fulfilment, and sense of meaning and community belonging felt by simple livers prior to adopting voluntary simplicity are attributed to the life style associated with the dominant culture … They don't realize that the fact that they can pass as mainstream … means they have privilege over many in society who can't' (2004:162).

Etzioni uses Maslow's hierarchy to explain why Voluntary Simplicity is a movement populated by the more privileged members of society, those whose basic needs are satisfied and who can be assured they will be met into the future, and therefore can concentrate on the highest point of the pyramid – that of self-actualisation. This, he argues, is why Voluntary Simplicity is a choice for lawyers, but not for homeless people (1998:632). This is a welcome attempt to take Maslow back from the world of marketing in which it is so frequently used and in which it is suggested consumer goods can aid self-actualisation if only they are well-enough designed. However, it does suggest that a person who does not have suitable shelter or the security of knowing they will have enough food never has any other kinds of needs. Not only is this untrue, but it negates the actual experiences of those in poverty, many of whom in developed countries have fallen into poverty from various trajectories. This is especially the case since austerity measures were introduced in the UK; food banks are *not* typically used by people who could be classed as long-standing members of the most deprived working classes.

Conclusion: Thoreau in the city

The title of this book is not only descriptive, but wilfully creative of a new history. Thrift has tended to be portrayed in historical and economic discourse as either a 'new movement', or as something that has occurred in historical 'blips' or 'moments' when historical conditions impacted negatively upon capitalism's ability to provide. There is so much wrong with this interpretation that it is difficult to know where to begin! For a start, capitalism is not known for its ability to provide for all; rather for its ability to enrichen some and at best entail some form of 'trickle-down' of that wealth to others (although there is rightly much scepticism about this). So, it stands to reason that for many, in fact most, people on the planet thrift in the form of frugality is simply a fact of everyday life. Historical discourses that present it as something that only occurs when times are economically tough, or amongst those who have enough to cut back a little, fail to recognise the material reality of the majority world.[1]

In addition, this account assumes that capitalism forms some kind of unquestionable backdrop to economic history in which moments of thrift can only ever be that – moments – rather than a history in their own right; perhaps one that is constantly competing with capitalism, or indeed that has evolved dialectically with it. As Terrance Witkowski asserts, 'ignorance of anti-consumption history risks being more than just a lost analytical opportunity. Historical amnesia may conceivably lead to serious factual errors when, for example, naïve scholars believe their topic to be something new, perhaps an emerging trend or movement, when in reality it is just one further chapter in a long-running story' (2010:238).

Finally, a positing of history as essentially a history of the growth of capitalism also consistently displays a strong tendency to assume the unquestionable presence of Smith's economic man. He is, after all, the reason for capitalism's apparent smooth and continuous development. In contrast, reciprocal human beings have shown themselves in various geographical contexts to be making history to an equal, if not greater, extent. To be clear, this is not to posit some kind of overarching human nature that for sake of argument is more reciprocal than maximising – such essentialisms are precisely the problem with Smith and indeed any non-materialist account of economic history. Rather, insisting upon the reciprocal human is to insist that material conditions have created reactions of thrift and reciprocity to a far greater extent than a capitalist economic history is prepared to admit. So, to begin this conclusion, three things can be said: thrift as frugality is simply daily reality for the majority of the world's population; thrift (as frugality and thriving) does not constitute 'moments' in a smooth trajectory of capitalism; thrift (as thriving, and even in some cases as frugality) proves that material conditions are just as likely to result in reciprocity than maximisation. Therefore, this book attempts to make a small start towards re-thinking the concept of thrift, both in terms of attempting to remove it from frugality per se (as its primary principle or motivation) and in terms of attempting to prove it can be used to carve out future alternatives, not simply shore up existing systems.

To be sure, writing a history of thrift as thriving rather entails writing a 'Left' history whether one means to or not, as the thrift that has resisted frugality has almost always adhered to what could broadly be agreed to be Left-wing thinking. It becomes about reclaiming thrift for the Left regardless of one's primary motivation. This is no simple task, as many if not most on the political Left have understandably despised thrift (as frugality) historically. Perhaps most famously, Oscar Wilde's previously quoted take on it is worth repeating here: 'to recommend thrift to the poor is both grotesque and insulting. It is like advising a man who is starving to eat less' (2001). Similarly, in his address to the British TUC, John Burns insisted 'Thrift was invented by capitalist rogues to beguile fools to destruction, and to deprive honest fools of their diet and their proper comfort' (1894). William Morris too was strongly anti-thrift, describing 'preachments of thrift to lack-alls', as part of a set of 'partial revolts' by 'a vast wide-spreading grasping organization' that he felt would 'meet every attempt at bettering the condition of the people' (1884). Maria Ossowaska describes thrift as 'that sovereign bourgeois virtue' (1986). Belfort Bax, the well-known socialist leader of the Victorian era, saw thrift as part of capitalism, arguing 'the aim of the Socialist therefore, which is the enjoyment of the products of labour as opposed to that of the bourgeois which is their mere accumulation with a view to "surplus-value", is radically at variance with "thrift"' (1884). This class angle on thrift was arguably best articulated by Algernon Sidney Crapsey, in *The Rise of the Working Class*: 'When one class is subject to another class, the thrift of the subject class only adds to the wealth of the master class ... [this is why] in the morality of the working class the word thrift will not be found' (1914).

Marx himself was also, not surprisingly, against thrift (as frugality), describing political economy as a 'science of wealth' whose 'true ideal is the ascetic but productive slave'. He goes on to say, 'Its moral idea is the worker who puts a part of his wages into savings ... The less you eat, drink, buy books, go to the theatre, go dancing, go drinking, think, love, theorize, sing, paint, fence, etc., the more you save and the greater will become the treasure that neither moths nor maggots can consume – your capital ... Everything which the political economist takes from you in terms of life and humanity, he restores to you in the form of money and wealth' (1961). Of course, in a far wider sense, Marxism entirely lends itself to the practice of thrift as thriving, and to ways of living that take back control of the means of production, hence his influence on Thoreau and his place in a Left history of thrift. Indeed, such concerns about avarice are reminiscent of Thoreau's concern over the Brook Farm experiment that was explored in the chapter on spiritual thrift.

However, this disdain for thrift on the part of the Left is precisely due to its being re-appropriated, mainly by Centre-Right or Right-wing thinkers throughout history who have focused on frugality rather than thriving. As Yates and Hunter argue, there is compelling evidence to suggest that a new thrift ethic is mobilising. As they say, 'We may very well live at the end of thrift. However, we may also be living between dominant forms of thrift ... we too may be on the verge of a new hegemonic form of the thrift ethos' (2011:9). Recent discourses on de-growth and their interaction with certain thinking on post-development is testament to this. In addition, such thinking is not simply zeitgeist rhetoric without historical foundation – it has its own history. Furthermore, this history cannot fail to assert the presence of reciprocal humans.

The charting of this history requires a proper in-depth philosophical analysis of the linkages between different thinkers, and cannot be attempted here. However, suffice to say, de-growth and its practical application in movements such as Voluntary Simplicity cannot be removed from the specific set of ecological and political concerns that informed Thoreau's sojourn in the woods of Walden Pond. Many voluntary simplifiers cite Thoreau as their inspiration, as previously mentioned studies have shown. Thoreau himself of course was avowedly concerned, to the detriment of all other pursuits in life, with thriving and living life in all its minute detail as an exercise in personal autonomy against capitalistic systems. Needless to say, Thoreau was influenced by Marx as much as Darwin or the transcendentalists, and practiced frugality as a means to his greatest thriving, rather than as a way to play his part in a specific economy or by specific economic rules. His insistence on thriving can usefully be spoken about in light of Aristotle's eudaimonia or 'human flourishing'. This is not to make of this book an exercise in tracing all Western concepts back to a Greek philosopher (as is too often engaged upon), but simply to usefully trace pieces of political thought and influence.

It is, therefore, with no apology that this book chooses to title its conclusion after Thoreau and indeed to base its concluding vision on his. Less so *Walden*, but certainly *Wild Fruits*, provide the beginnings of a blueprint for de-growth society. Thoreau insists upon collectivity for the sake of the collective, rather than as part of a market system. This is seen in his response to the Brook Farm experiment, and can be usefully related to current discourses on de-growth that promote simply leaving the market. However, his writings are, admittedly, rather steeped in melancholic nostalgia for an already-fading agrarian age. They are also, therefore, avowedly rural in terms of the blueprint they provide. The work then to be done here is to take Thoreau's blueprint and take it to the city as it were. The vision this book would like to suggest is neither nostalgic nor rural. It has no Luddite tendencies, nor does it require any kind of 'return' to former values of structures. It is quintessentially forward-looking, urban-inspired (if not simply urban) and digital. It is, as admitted in the introduction too, unapologetically idealist, but it is not alone in this. Many current authors engaging with the growing body of literature on the Anthropocene are insisting that it is entirely appropriate at this historical juncture to engage in idealism – what else, after all, is to be done, when one begins to imagine a new and entirely different future? If there is utopianism at play (although the discerning reader will realise it is hopeful realism in actual fact), it is because at the present historical juncture there is little to lose, in fact there is no alternative. This book, and indeed all those who are currently discussing these issues, are naive in a knowing way – a stance one might usefully call *wilful naivety*.

There are a number of aspects that are key to this vision, and what follows will provide a brief explanation and thinking on each. First, the new society of thrift as thriving requires collective commodities and a solid commitment to maintaining them as collective. By collective commodities what is meant is those goods and services provisioned and consumed primarily by individuals and those that require mass provision, most usually through the state, such as public transport and mass education services. The term was developed by Manuel Castells in his 1977 book, *The Urban Question*, as a critical concept for explaining urban change in the postwar era. Since then, thinkers such as Peter Saunders have argued that in terms of urban consumption, the main division that has emerged due to capitalism is between those who satisfy their requirements through personal ownership of commodities (i.e. private consumption) and those who rely upon state provision (i.e. collective consumption). It is this 'consumption cleavage' that has become the principal source of division in consumer societies according to Saunders. It is also this that any society based on thrift as thriving would need to address; from both a reciprocity and an ecological perspective the sheer level of ownership of private goods must be lessened.

There is a problem with a straightforward embracing of collective goods though, and that is that they tend inherently to be the products of the state, and the place and power of the state in a society of thrift as thriving is one that will require very careful consideration. One issue that therefore needs addressing is whether collective commodities can exist easily and frequently enough without being state products. Is it possible to get beyond car-sharing and neighbourhood self-organised school runs without the hand of the state? If not, what ought to be the involvement of the state, and how can a society of thrift avoid the worst pitfalls of David Cameron's proposed 'Big Society'. These are large and important questions that future work hopes to address.

In many ways, collective commodities require a new relationship between consumer and commodity in a sense not dissimilar to the promotion of 'socialist products' in the early stages of the USSR. Such objects were not only designed to make sure citizens were first and foremost socialists as opposed to consumers, but also aimed to fundamentally change the relationship between the subject and object. Their conception and design were inspired by the 'constructivists' of the 1920s, most famous amongst whom was Boris Arvatov. Arvatov argued that re-thinking one's relation to commodities and objects was part of the overall transformation of everyday life that came along with revolutionary change. Key to his thinking was the idea that in order for commodities not to be capitalist, they should be seen as *active*, in other words, understood as fundamentally functional and active rather than simply acted upon by consumers, and therefore 'connected like a co-worker with human practice' (1997:26). For Arvatov, objects should not be seen as 'dead', but rather as part of a 'systematically regulated dynamism of things' (1997:128). Or, as prominent Constructivist Alexander Rodchenko put it, 'our things in our hands must be also equals, also comrades' (Rodchenko *et al.*, 1991). It was only as co-workers, alongside socialist subjects, that commodities could resist the fetishisation of capitalism and be part of shaping a socialist reality. In fact, as Christina Kiaer argues, rather than trying to dispel the power of the commodity fetish, the constructivists tried to confront it and reclaim it for socialism (2005:90). As Stephen Shukaitis argues, they strove to 'break the spell of the commodity whilst retaining it as a site of individual and collective formation of fantasy' (2013:440).

Importantly, such objects would not only resist being fetishised as capitalist objects, but would also, in their role as co-workers, actually 'produce' (socialist) human subjects (Arvatov, 1997:126). To put this in rather more practical perspective, socialist objects were often designed with functionality as their primary function (such as dresses with large useful pockets), and in ways that meant they had double uses or could be repurposed throughout their life-cycle (such as children's toys that could be reconfigured to grow with the child). Such objects, it was thought, would teach subjects how to use them in ways aligned to socialist thinking. In many cases, they promoted a longer life-cycle and a thrifty use of resources. As ethereal as the ideas behind socialist objects might seem, there is perhaps much to learn from them in creating a current-day thrift based on thriving.

In addition to creating collective commodities, the ethos of collectivity in a society of thrift as thriving needs to lessen the need for individualism and therefore create new solidarities – not of consumer tribes, but of mutually supportive connections. The 'reciprocity work' talked of by de-growth theorists will be key in this task, and need to be powerful enough to render existing 'support' facilities irrelevant. This in turn will see the end of financialisation of essential services, for example the destruction of paid-for childcare services.

Both the above aspects will require the presence of the (avowedly urban) form of the agora (from the ancient Greek), which can best be understood as a central public space. The literal meaning of the word is 'gathering place' or 'assembly', but in practice the agora was far more than that, becoming the athletic, artistic, spiritual and political life of the city. Importantly, the agora is not primarily a market or place of financial exchange, therefore, choosing to use this word enables a reimagining of the market as a space that embodies civil obligation and participation. In short, it demands of the citizen that they behave as a reciprocal person, rather than simply as 'economic man'. As Latouche argues, the form of the agora re-inscribes exchange within the social and the political and means 'markets' have social and political functions (2003). This means embedding the agora within local contexts so that the reality of its products and presence is more immediate to those who take part it in. In this sense, the agora fits the localisation aspect of de-growth thinking as it must attempt to produce locally most of the products the population it serves require if it is to fulfil its political and social awareness function.

These aspects effectively bring together elements of thrift as thriving that have already stood the test of history. They prove that capitalism was not the backdrop to all history, everywhere, all the time, regardless of its huge and undeniable impact. They also prove the presence of reciprocal human beings. Cooperating persons in many ways are far more autonomous; they have what Bernard Stiegler calls 'savoir vivre'. The concept of 'savoir vivre' was first developed by Stiegler in the three volumes of his *Mécréance et Discrédit* (2004, 2006a, 2006b). These volumes outlined the way in which the industrial organisation of production and then consumption has had destructive consequences for the modes of life of human beings, in particular with the way in which the loss of savoir faire and savoir vivre (that is, the loss of the knowledge of how to do and how to live) has resulted in what Stiegler calls 'generalised proletarianisation'. In an interview with Patrick Crogan, Stiegler interprets Marx's definition of the proletariat as not being about pauperisation, but rather as resting upon the de-skilling of the worker (Crogan, 2010:161). (Marx describes the proletariat as a worker who had skills and savoir faire, but who has been dispossessed of them by the introduction of machines.) Stiegler points out that this is also precisely what Adam Smith had said almost a century earlier in *The Wealth of Nations* (Stiegler, 2004), but he had not made a political theory out of it. Similarly, Gilbert Simondon has called this de-skilling disindividuation, based on the logic that when individuation comes through the singular knowledge a person possesses, if this is taken away from them they are disindividualised (2017). For Stiegler, the same process of proletarianisation that the worker experienced has also now rendered the consumer less capable of knowing how to live (savoir vivre). He argues, 'from the moment when marketing invents the service society ... we see how the consumer is himself deprived of his savoir vivre. The producer was deprived of his skills or abilities (savoir faire), the consumer is deprived of his savoir vivre' (Crogan, 2010:161).

Thus, according to Stiegler, the proletariat consumer is left with nothing but his purchasing power, just as the proletariat producer was left with nothing but his labour power – 'so he will work to earn the little bit of money he uses to be able to buy what he produces, having lost everything; he has no knowledge in work anymore and no knowledge in life. So he is unhappy' (Crogan, 2010:162). Furthermore, Stiegler's vision of the disempowered consumer is instrumental in placing the (already dispossessed) worker as a (now dispossessed) consumer, who can do nothing but attempt to gain pleasure in spending on the most ephemeral and inexpensive of commodities. What Stiegler posits as a replacement to this is a world in which rather than there being consumers on one side and producers on the other, there are simply 'contributors' who 'participate in the creation of the world in which they live' – a world which could be described as 'open source' (Crogan, 2010:162). With a resurgence of savoir vivre, then, reciprocal humans not only replace the literal and theoretical presence of economic man, but in doing so force a broadening of the consumption debate. Reciprocal humans are not simply consumer (or non-consumers), but humans who can only be considered in light of all human activities. Talking about consumption and thrift becomes talking about not only how we as individuals might wish to live, but about entire development trajectories.

The introduction to this book explained that the shift from thrift as thriving (ethical shift) to thrift as frugality (moral thrift) meant it has been gradually prised away from actually *belonging* to people as a practice of everyday life. Practices that enable cheap living are at worst increasingly scorned and eradicated, at best bureaucratised, and in the process are effectively made unfeasible for the numbers of people previously engaging in them. In reality, attempts at thrift are only condoned by governments in the West if they are still generative of profit, despite the ways in which they may enable individuals to move on from precisely the kinds of poverty traps that do disallow them to be full citizens, contributing (financially or otherwise) to society. The commercialising of thrift disavows it of its creativity and (ironically) of its self-reliance and economic resilience. Thrift of the non-taxable, non-consumptive variety, then, becomes presented in much the same way as those on long-term benefits, gypsies and other 'off-grid' communities – it is the austerity that, unlike its government-sponsored other, cannot speak its name.

So, in addition to providing a blueprint for future attempts to thrive, the arguments in the preceding paragraphs are also an attempt to suggest the elements of thrift thinking that might enable it to be fully recaptured by people (as opposed to growth-hungry governments and corporations) and to return to its ethical sense. This is to make of thrift a resistant practice. Resistant, not necessarily in a clichéd anti-capitalist way, but in a way that genuinely seeks huge changes in the logic behind society's running. Key to this idealism and wilful naivety is the desire and vision to remove thrift from moralising individualistic rationales and make it more communal; in short, to make it a tool in new structures of social solidarity.

The reclamation of thrift must, then, be one that removes it from moralistic historical discourses – both early modern and contemporary. Its linkages to 'moral behaviour', whether through wartime frugality, postwar consumer individualism or current-day household economia have caused it to be too easily hijacked by the predominant political thought of the day, and too easily linked to the concept of duty. The role of thrift now could, and this book argues *should*, be precisely to resist, disrupt and refuse the political tide that financialises ever-greater areas of everyday life whilst cutting back provision in areas previously considered sacrosanct in terms of the necessity for them to be universal and free for all. To strip thrift of its moral potency is actually to give it a far greater role to play in societal change – a role of creating new solidarities rather than individualism; or resistance rather than top-down morality. It is, effectively, to reclaim it as an *ethical* concept rather than a moral one; one that enables an informed pursuit of a way of life. Inevitably, this shift from morality to ethicality necessarily involves the move from economic man to reciprocal man; a move that, as previously mentioned, is not a challenge against some kind of 'natural' way of being, but rather that allows in a mode of being that has been refused, legislated against and persecuted throughout the neoliberal era.

It is crucial to acknowledge, finally, that this thrift-as-thriving still, admittedly, addresses itself to those in the developed world who, essentially, can manage to live differently. Such has been the nature of thrift discourses and practice (both as thriving and frugality) throughout history. So, this book is not simply a purportedly more radical demand for the poor to give up what they already do not have. In fact, addressing thrift to the developed world and framing it in specific bodies of work on post-development make it, finally, about a more global vision, and precisely about asking the 'haves' to change in order that the 'have nots' can have improved lives.

There are indeed many advantages for those who can afford it, to working less, being more self-sufficient, gaining more time and living, as Thoreau put it, more 'deliberately'. One of the major problems with thrift is precisely its emphasis on individual happiness, to be acquired through *economic* freedom or the quietening of needs. This is essentially a position, despite its often anti-capitalist credentials, that taps into capitalistic logic and does nothing to challenge inequality. It shows echoes of Benedetto Croce's insistence that inequality was absurd and impossible – a position that essentially backs neoliberalism.[2] This desire for happiness via *economic* freedom, whilst valid, is not enough. Thrift needs to also be an attempt at happiness that requires greater equality within society. Essentially, only the Left history of thrift has ever challenged this. The more known-about history of thrift has simply asked those who earn little to manage their money better, and those who have plenty to decide they require a little less. This is hardly the promotion of the reallocation of resources on a societal level.

Such logic, however, is no longer the driving force behind thrift as thriving. Global issues such as the ecological imperative of the Anthropocene and the potential for new economic systems and far greater global equality are at stake. This is precisely to take thrift out of the hands of those who can afford to be thrifty; and to engage them in a collective process that empowers those who cannot afford to be (for whom thrift is simply normality). Thoreau's issue with Brook Farm was precisely that, and whilst his answer may have at first appeared individualistic, by the end of his life he had attempted to come up with an alternative collective thrift that bypassed the mechanisms of capitalism and challenged economic inequality. So, to return thrift to thriving is not simply about the personal happiness of the middle-class few, but about equality. Thrift (as both thriving and frugality) has been sold repeatedly throughout history to those who cannot afford it and who have been made to feel personally responsible for their own and society's lack of resources. What is required is a thrift that is relevant and practice-able for all, that sets up collectivity as a leveller, and as a form of societal provision. In many ways the ecological imperative thrown up by acknowledging the Anthropocene enables a helpful escape from the kind of morality on consumption that the Frankfurt School brought about, and creates a genuinely ethical motivation for living differently with thrift. And, with Escobar, this living differently is about everyone developing along brand new trajectories, rendering irrelevant issues of at what point in development can a society be reasonable expected to simplify and who stands to benefit if it does. Carefully drawn away from its capitalist applications, thrift becomes just such a weapon-concept as is needed in creating these new developmental trajectories.

Afterword

I admitted in the preface to this book that I felt my relationship to thrift (even thrift as thriving) was essentially at best complicated, and at worst hypocritical. Having engaged with the thinkers in this book as I wrote, it now occurs to me that my position is actually perhaps something I can live with more happily than I thought! I have, unwittingly, been living as simply as possible for over a decade. I have never accumulated much stuff (and that remains the case even now that I have a child). I have always tried to remain in control of my time as far as was possible and despite very average earnings have had very few periods when I carried out work that made me unhappy in a full-time position. (Although there were plenty of times I sacrificed work satisfaction to earn enough in a short space of time to buy my freedom!) I have never owned a car. I have not owned a television for about fifteen years now and have avoided much commercial (in particular celebrity) culture. I am not a hermit. I live in a city, I have a relatively mainstream life, a mortgage, a job, I am aware of new figures in popular culture and new TV formats (well – the ones you couldn't miss anyway). But I realise that I have simplified without becoming a simplifier! And I am very glad. I also realise, that because I had not realised I was a simplifier, that this was not done as some kind of anti-capitalist protest. Don't get me wrong, I do strongly believe many aspects of a capitalist system make for a less just and fulfilling life for most people, but my own choices in how to live were not explicitly about that – I just liked the simplicity and most of all the sense of not needing much. It made me feel free, and able to take hard times on the chin as it were. All of this is classic privileged simplifier stuff in some ways, and I recognise this, but engaging with scholarly work on the Anthropocene and de-growth has caused me to realise that promoting thrift as thriving is not something I need to feel slightly embarrassed about due to my own awkwardness over not wanting to be preachy. Rather, this is a far wider concern with the development trajectories of societies across the globe. Movements in the developing world have rendered less relevant concerns that only the rich can employ thrift as thriving; they have made thrift about other factors such as power, agency, self-sufficiency and reciprocity.

Notes

1 Towards a theory of thrift

1 In addition, however, Miller (2013) challenges the existing notions of thrift as a means to an end via short-term sacrifice, arguing that thrift can also be an autotelic activity.
2 J. K. Gibson-Graham is a pen name shared by feminist economic geographers Julie Graham and Katherine Gibson.
3 For many consumers in the developed world acknowledging the exploitation of developing world labour leads to a commitment to ethical consumption. There is no room or need to enter into the pros and cons of ethical consumption here, suffice to say that 'sustainable' goods often come with a higher price tag and thus are often beyond the financial reach of those on the lowest incomes. This is essentially the well-documented issue that ethical consumption is only possible for the middle classes; it is incompatible with thrift as frugality.

2 Religious thrift: Puritans, Quakers and Methodists

1 The Puritans were a group of English Reformed Protestants in the sixteenth and seventeenth centuries who sought to *purify* the Church of England from all Catholic practices. Historically, 'Puritan' was a pejorative term used by critics of the group to characterise them as extremists. Some of these English Puritans travelled to America, taking the thinking to New England.
2 The term 'economic man' is usually attributed to eighteenth-century thinkers Adam Smith and David Ricardo, although has its origins in much earlier thinkers such as Mandeville. In the nineteenth century, John Stuart Mill built on the concept, explaining that economic man was one who 'inevitably does that by which he may obtain the greatest amount of necessaries, conveniences, and luxuries, with the smallest quantity of labour and physical self-denial with which they can be obtained' (Mill, 1844).
3 Quakers is the name more commonly given to the Religious Society of Friends, and came about due to the Founder George Fox telling people to 'tremble (or quake) at the word of the Lord'.
4 George Fox famously climbed Pendle Hill in Lancashire in June of 1652, where he had a vision of many souls coming to Christ. This moment is generally accepted as the 'beginning' of Quakerism, although Fox had been preaching for some years beforehand, and continued to do so with even greater vigour afterwards.
5 William Penn (1644–1718) was an English landowner, philosopher and early advocate of democracy and religious freedom. In 1681 King Charles II handed over a large piece of his American land holdings to William Penn to satisfy a debt the king owed to Penn's father. This land included present-day Pennsylvania and Delaware. Penn arrived in America in 1682 and set up his new colony. Afterwards, Penn journeyed up the Delaware River and founded Philadelphia. It was under his direction that the city of Philadelphia was planned and developed.

6 The Testimony of Simplicity is a shorthand description of the actions generally taken by Quakers to *testify* or *bear witness* to their beliefs that a person ought to live a simple life.
7 Quakernomics is a form of ethical capitalism. Its current practice and history are very well explored by Mike King in *Quakernomics* (2014).
8 The Great Awakening (sometimes referred to as the First Great Awakening or the Evangelical Revival) was a period of Christian revivals across Britain and its colonies during the 1730s and 1740s. It drew upon older traditions such as Puritanism. Those involved were keen to renew individual piety and religious devotion.
9 Arminius had been trained to preach Calvinism, but he opposed many of its teachings and believed that *some* aspects of Calvinism had to be modified in the light of Scripture. His name spawned *Arminianism*, which is seen as the insistence on the role of free will in salvation, against the idea of predestination.
10 *The Making of the English Working Class* explores English social history and is considered part of the 'New Left' movements of the 1960s. It concentrates on English working-class society in what Thompson considered to be its formative years – from 1780 to 1832. He sought to challenge what he saw as a patronising portrayal of artisans and makers, and believed the generation of Methodists that followed Wesley's death in 1791 to have facilitated dehumanising industrialisation and political repression. Many more recent commentators have criticised Thompson for a 'romantic' and 'nostalgic' portrayal of the artisan working class (see, for example, Owen Hatherley's *Ministry of Nostalgia*, 2016).
11 The Parable of the Talents is one of the well-known parables of Jesus Christ. It appears in the Bible in Matthew 25:14–30.
12 In *Capital*, volume one, chapter 10, Marx talks of capitalists as 'vampires' sucking the blood of the workers: 'The contract by which he sold to the capitalist his labour-power proved, so to say, in black and white that he disposed of himself freely. The bargain concluded, it is discovered that he was no "free agent," that the time for which he is free to sell his labour-power is the time for which he is forced to sell it, that in fact the vampire will not lose its hold on him so long as there is a muscle, a nerve, a drop of blood to be exploited.'
13 Paul waived his right, as an apostle, to be supported financially by those to whom he was ministering. He preached at no cost to the Corinthians so as not to hinder the message of the gospel (see Corinthians 9:1–23), working as a tentmaker to survive. When he finally ministered full-time to the Corinthians, it was thanks to the financial support of the Macedonians (see Acts 18:1–5; Coronthians 11:7–9; Philippians 4:15, 18). Paul was essentially motivated by the desire not to be a burden financially.

3 Individualist thrift: Benjamin Franklin, Samuel Smiles and Victorian moralism

1 Franklin is credited with inventing, amongst other things, the lightning rod, the Franklin stove, bifocal glasses and the flexible urinary catheter. He never patented his inventions, believing they should be free for everyone to use.
2 Franklin's most famous writings were *Poor Richard's Almanack* (1732–1757) and *The Way to Wealth* (1757).

3   Franklin published his views as Articles of Belief and Acts of Religion, 1728. They can be found at franklinpapers.org/franklin/framedVolumes.jsp?vol=1&page=101a
4   The name Richard Saunders was borrowed from the seventeenth-century author of a popular London almanac entitled *Rider's British Merlin* and the persona was based in part on Jonathan Swift's character Issac Bickerstaff.
5   In Franklin's era there was widespread debt due to the necessity to borrow money in order to make a living. For example, merchants in New England, Pennsylvania and Chesapeake colonies often sold as much as 80–90 per cent of their goods on credit. In addition, the colonies were locked into a highly interdependent system of commercial relationships that depended on credit, yet the penalties for being over-indebted were harsh and could easily result in imprisonment alongside those who had committed serious and violent crimes.
6   Eudaimonia (sometimes eudaemonia or eudemonia) is a Greek word most usually translated as happiness. Etymologically, it consists of the words *eu* ('good') and *daimon* ('spirit').
7   This is obviously a highly cursory glance into Aristotle's concept. A return to the original texts – *Nicomachean Ethics* and the *Eudemian Ethics* – would provide more depth for the interested reader.
8   This is Harriet Beecher Stowe who famously wrote *Uncle Tom's Cabin*.
9   Incidentally, Mr (Wilkins) Micawber was modelled on Dickens' father, John Dickens, who like Micawber was incarcerated in debtors' prison after failing to meet his creditors' demands.
10 Wharton herself was an unlikely character to write about thrift. Born in 1862 and raised in upper-class New York society, she was by mid-career the highest paid living novelist in the United States. She owned several magnificent homes, employed servants, travelled incessantly, entertained frequently, and lived a life of ease.
11 Smiles wrote: *Self-Help* (1859); *Character* (1871); *Thrift* (1875); *Duty* (1880); and *Life and Labour* (1887).
12 Cameronians followed the teachings of Richard Cameron, leader of the militant Presbyterians or ('Convenanters') who resisted attempts by the Stuart monarchs to control the affairs of the Church of Scotland. Frustrated with the English king's acceptance of Roman Catholics, they became a separate church after the religious settlement of 1690. Due to their dissatisfaction with the moderate nature of the religious settlement they were seen as narrow-minded zealots. However, recent biographies have painted the Cameronians' struggle as one of religious and civil liberty in the face of a hereditary monarchy and therefore an expression of republicanism. Cameron's thought still resonates with recent and current generations of Scottish Protestants. Although Smiles was not a practising Cameronian, his moralism can clearly be seen as Presbyterian, despite being slightly more benign than many of his contemporaries.
13 On 7 December 1843, Samuel married Sarah Ann Holmes Dixon in Leeds. They had three daughters, Janet, Edith and Lillian, and two sons, William and Samuel. Smiles' grandchildren include Sir Walter Smiles, an Ulster Unionist Party MP. Smiles is also the great-great-grandfather of the explorer Bear Grylls. He died aged ninety-four in 1904.
14 Augustine defined perseverance as a special gift from God, based on the rationale that only those graced by God can persevere in faith to the end of their lives. He thus united the idea of godliness with that of a life of unceasing toil, as a person could fall from grace even if they stopped persevering a moment before their death. Calvin's version followed Augustine's in most points, but asserted that a believer could become sure of having received God's grace before dying.

15 Transcendentalism is a philosophical movement that developed in the late 1820s and 1830s in the eastern United States, in response to the rise of Unitarian doctrine. It emerged from English and German romanticism, biblical criticism, the scepticism of Hume and the transcendental philosophy of Kant. It also took much from Hindu texts on philosophy of the mind and spirituality. A core belief of transcendentalism is in the inherent goodness of people and nature. Adherents believe that society and its institutions have corrupted the purity of the individual, and they have faith that people are at their best when truly self-reliant.
16 See BBC (2016).
17 See Benedict Brogan's interview with Boris Johnson in the *Telegraph* (Brogan, 2010).
18 One Nationism is a form of British Conservativism, rooted in paternalistic views, and that believes itself to be committed to the narrowing of the gap between rich and poor.
19 Disraeli's reigns were sandwiched between those of his great rival William Gladstone. He was prime minister of Britain twice – once in 1868, and once from 1874 to 1880.
20 Functionalism was a sociological perspective that emerged from the American sociologist Talcott Parsons (1902–1979). It saw society as a complex system consisting of various parts that worked together to promote stability. Since the 1970s, Parsons' theories have been robustly critiqued as socially conservative.
21 Charles Alan Murray (1943–present) is an American libertarian political scientist, author, columnist and pundit. He became well known for his *Losing Ground: American Social Policy 1950–1980*, published in 1984, which discussed the American welfare system, and has written many controversial books since.
22 The New Right describes international thinking that was in favour of liberal economic policies and a decline in state intervention. In the UK, it was typified by Margaret Thatcher who insisted on the necessity of reviving individualism and challenging the 'dependency culture' apparently created by the welfare state. In the United States, its equivalent proponent at the time was President Ronald Reagan.
23 There was a brief return to One Nation politics during the interwar period due to fears of communism and popular Left sentiment. In Britain, this influenced the creation of a welfare state and National Health Service following the Second World War, factors that were key in the postwar consensus of the 1950s and 1960s.

4 Spiritual thrift: simplicity, sensuality and politics in Henry Thoreau

1 See Adams (1945).
2 Emerson (1803–1882) is a famous American essayist, lecturer and poet. He led the transcendentalist movement of the mid-nineteenth century.
3 Briefly, transcendentalism emerged from a confluence of English and German romanticism, the biblical criticism of Johann Gottfried Herder and Friedrich Schleiermacher, the scepticism of David Hume, and the transcendental philosophy of Immanuel Kant. It was also influenced by Hindu texts on philosophy of the mind and spirituality. Its key beliefs were in the inherent goodness of people and nature, and the corruption of these by society and its institutions. Transcendentalism held that people are at their best when truly self-reliant. It placed emphasis on subjective intuition over objective empiricism and its adherents believed that individuals were capable of generating completely original insights with as little attention and deference to past masters as possible.

4 Thoreau was a lifelong abolitionist, and gave many lectures attacking the Fugitive Slave Law. He publicly praised the writings of abolitionists such as Wendell Phillips and John Brown.
5 In actual fact, this 'year' was the way in which Thoreau chose to recount the two years, two months, and two days he had spent at Walden. During this period, he had left Walden now and then for short periods. The book, *Walden*, compresses that time into a single calendar year, using the passage of the four seasons to symbolise human development.
6 The word comes from satya: '*truth*', agraha: '*insistence*' or '*holding firmly to*'. 'Holding onto truth' is a particular form of non-violent resistance or civil resistance coined by Gandhi and used in his own struggles and those of the civil right movements in the United States.
7 See George Hendrick's 1956 article 'The Influence of Thoreau's "Civil Disobedience" on Gandhi's Satyagraha' for further explanation of this influence and the timings involved.
8 This was originally published as 'Resistance to Civil Government' in 1849. Thoreau was motivated to write it in large part by his disgust with slavery and the Mexican–American War (1846–1848).
9 Etzler's manifesto was entitled *Paradise within the Reach of all Men, without Labor, by Powers of Nature and Machinery* (1842).
10 There is evidence that Thoreau visited Brook Farm on 3 December 1843, in the form of a letter discovered by Sterling Delano, in which a Brook Farm resident – George Bradford – inquires after Thoreau, regretting that he had let him depart in an omnibus during a snow storm considering his delicate health (see Newman, 2003:516).
11 At the height of the electioneering, Orestes Brownson published 'The Laboring Classes', in which he argued for a radical change in all social arrangements, including the outlawing of all inheritance of private property, and asserted that if such a law was not passed there would be social revolution. This alienated the Boston intellectuals, and despite Brownson's attempts to make his loyalty to them clear, Whig journalists across the country convinced many that the article revealed the true plans of the Democrats.
12 The Association movement was extremely strong in the 1840s. Periodicals of the time contain much debate about it, the *New York Tribune* carried a front-page column on it for a year and a half, and Parke Godwin's *Popular View of the Doctrines of Charles Fourier* was widely circulated. Some estimates of the number of Associationists and their active supporters are as high as 100,000. Members ranged from farmers and mechanics, to lawyers, merchants, doctors, shopkeepers, ministers and writers. Associationism was a serious challenge to the course of capitalism.
13 This manuscript passed through several collections for a century and a half after being found shortly after Thoreau's death, but has only recently been published.

5 Nationalist thrift: making do, rationing and nostalgic austerity

1 The motives for this may not have been straightforward, however. A survey in *The Economist*, published in 1942, showed that only one-fifth of allotment holders claimed to be working them to help the war effort. Over half said their main aim was to produce

fresh food for themselves, family and friends, and about one-fifth cited 'fresh air' and the desire 'to save money' as their chief objectives (see Briggs, 2000: 59).
2 The BBC radio comedy *It's That Man Again* ran from 1939 to 1949. The title refers to a contemporary phrase concerning the ever more frequent news stories about Hitler in the lead-up to the Second World War, specifically a headline in the *Daily Express* newspaper written by Bert Gunn. ITMA was written by Ted Kavanagh and starred Tommy Handley. It was seen as playing a major role in maintaining morale on Britain's 'home front' during the Second World War.
3 ITMA was originally set in a pirate radio station. Four episodes were broadcast over a trial period but were not overly successful. It wasn't until the re-launch of the programme after war had broken out that it was re-set in the 'Office of Twerps', where Tommy Handley's character was to become 'Minister of Aggravation and Mysteries'.
4 The A Side of the record was Tommy Handley and Dorothy Summers (aka Mrs Mopp) in a comedy sketch called 'Mrs. Mopp Joins The Home Guard' with Tommy as Mayor Handley of Foaming-at-the-Mouth, the contemporary setting for the series of ITMA at that time. The B Side was for the British Commercial Electrical Development Association and featured Jeanne de Casalis as Mrs Feather in 'Electric Harmony' on the phone to Mayor Handley as a resident of 'Foaming-at-the-Mouth'.
5 It is well known, but worth mentioning, that rationing led to a much improved national diet overall as working-class people ate better under rationing than they had previously been able to.
6 Make do and mend was a Second World War slogan devised by the wartime Board of Trade that encouraged housewives to consume less. Various booklets with tips on how to re-use and patch up objects were issued.
7 See Hulme (2016).
8 See www.energysavingtrust.org.uk/Media/Corporate-Media/Media-centreimages-docs/Wartime-spirit-campaign/Wartime-spirit-press-release. Accessed 20 September 2010.
9 The term 'Age-of-Austerity' (when used to refer to current times) was popularised by British Conservative leader David Cameron in his keynote speech to the Conservative Party forum in Cheltenham on 26 April 2009, in which he insisted upon the necessity of decreasing government spending.
10 Chancellor-to-be George Osborne said in his now much-quoted speech to the Conservative Party in 2009: 'These are the honest choices in the world in which we live and we have made them today. Anyone who tells you these choices can be avoided is not telling you the truth. We are all in this together.' See http://news.bbc.co.uk/1/hi/8292680.stm for details of the speech.

6 Consumer thrift: Keynes, consumer rights and the new thrifty consumers

1 Herbert Clark Hoover (1874–1964) was the 31st President of the United States, from 1929 to 1933. He was defeated by the Democrat Franklin D. Roosevelt.
2 This was financed by Johnson Publishing Company to encourage advertisers to promote their products and services in the African-American media. It showed

African-American professionals, housewives and students as participants in the American consumer society, emphasising their economic power and reliability when it came to paying up. The documentary aimed to show corporate America how to exploit African American's annual spending.
3 Rael argues thrift was even used to justify slavery and that the national discourse of thrift fragmented at this time as the North and South developed competing notions of it reflecting their differing economic situations. Whilst the North emphasised the bourgeois work ethic, industrialisation and urban life, the South stressed a conception rooted in an agricultural and slave-based economy (2011). For Yates and Hunter, in this way thrift not only enabled social control over subordinate groups (for example African-Americans and the poor), but also justified the wealth of the newly rich (2011:17).
4 Here Washington was in direct disagreement with W. E. B. Dubois, who said 'as far as Mr Washington apologizes for injustice ... does not rightly value the privileged and duty of voting, belittles the emasculating effects of caste distinctions, and opposes the higher training and ambitions of our brighter minds ... we must unceasingly and firmly oppose him' (W. E. B. Dubois, quoted in Blankenhorn, 2008).
5 In 1929 Robert and Helen Lynd wrote *Middletown: A Study in Contemporary American Culture*. It was primarily a look at changes in the white population of a 'typical' American city between 1890 and 1925. 'Middletown' was posited as a fictional city that was typical of many average US cities of its size. However, the residents of Muncie, Indiana, where the Lynds carried out their fieldwork, began to guess that their town had been the subject of the book. The Lynds returned to 'Middletown' (Muncie) in 1935 to research their second book – *Middletown in Transition: A Study in Cultural Conflicts* – which dealt with the ways in which the Great Depression might have changed the social structure of the town.
6 Jean-Baptiste Say (1767–1832) was a French liberal economist who argued in favour of competition, free trade and fewer constraints on business. Say's law is also known as the law of markets.

7 Ecological thrift: frugality, de-growth and Voluntary Simplicity

1 It is worth noting that, as with other studies of simplifiers (for example Elgin and Mitchell, 1977; Zavestoski, 2002; Pierce, 2003), the respondents to Huneke's survey were overwhelmingly female (73.5 per cent). They were roughly evenly divided among three age groups, 25–34 (21.2 per cent), 35–44 (28.3 per cent) and 45–54 (28.3 per cent), whereas 12.4 per cent were over fifty-five and 8 per cent under twenty-five. They were also more highly educated than the average American (more than 65 per cent holding at least a four-year degree), and came from higher than average income backgrounds (after adopting Voluntary Simplicity these respondents were still more likely than the average American to have a household income of $45,000 to $100,000, and less likely to have a household income under $45,000).
2 Of the 2,268 participants, 970 were from North America, 871 were from Australia, 147 were from the UK, 108 were from Western Europe (excluding the UK), 77 were from New Zealand, 4 were from Japan and 91 were from 'other' parts of the globe.

Conclusion: Thoreau in the city

1 The majority world is a term now frequently used in development discourses instead of the term 'developing world'. It aims to capture the fact that developing countries form the majority of the world's population. Subsequently, the 'developed world' is referred to as the 'minority world'. I choose to employ these terms throughout my teaching and writing.
2 See Ege and Igersheim's interpretation of Croce (2011).

References

Adams, R. (1945) 'Thoreau's Diploma', *American Literature*, vol. 17, Spring, pp. 174–175
Adatto, K. (2011) 'Saving for Democracy: Thrift, Sacrifice and the World War Two Bond Campaigns', in Yates, J. and Hunter, J. (eds) *Thrift and Thriving in America: Capitalism and the Moral Order from the Puritans to the Present*. New York: Oxford University Press
Aglietta, M. (1997) *Régulation et crises du capitalisme*. Paris: Editions Odile Jacob
Alexander, S. and Ussher, S. (2012) 'The Voluntary Simplicity Movement: A Multi-National Survey Analysis in Theoretical Context', *Journal of Consumer Culture*, vol. 12(1), pp. 66–86
Andreonia, V. and Galmarini, S. (2013) 'On the Increase of Social Capital in De-Growth Economy', *Procedia – Social and Behavioral Sciences*, vol. 72, pp. 64–72
Andrews, C. (1997) *The Circle of Simplicity: Return to the Good Life*. New York: HarperCollins
Angus, I. (2016) *Facing the Anthropocene*. New York: Monthly Review Press
Ariès, P. (2005) *Décroissance ou Barbarie*. Lyon: Golias
Aristotle (2009) *Politics*. Oxford: Oxford University Press
Arvatov, B. (1997) 'Everyday Life and the Culture of the Thing', *October*, vol. 81, pp. 119–128
Bainton, R. (1950) *Here I Stand: A Life of Martin Luther*. New York: Penguin Books
Ballaster, R., Beetham, M., Frazer, E. and Hebron, S. (1991) *Women's Worlds: Ideology, Femininity and the Woman's Magazine*. Basingstoke: Macmillan
Baltzell, E. (1996) *Puritan Boston and Quaker Philadelphia*. Piscataway: Transaction Publishers
Bardhi, F. and Arnould, E. (2005) 'Thrift Shopping: Combining Utilitarian Thrift and Hedonic Treat Benefits', *Journal of Consumer Behaviour*, vol. 4(4), pp. 223–233
Barton, Bruce (1926) *The Man Nobody Knows*. London: Constable & Co. Ltd
Bax, B. (1884) 'Unscientific Socialism', in Blankenhorn, D. (2008) *Thrift: A Cyclopedia Paperback*. New York: Templeton Foundation Press
BBC (2016) 'Theresa May Vows to be "One Nation" Prime Minister'. Available at: www.bbc.co.uk/news/uk-politics-36788782. Accessed 3 April 2017.
Bell, D. (1976) *The Cultural Contradictions of Capitalism*. New York: Basic Books
Bellamy, E. (2000) [1888] *Looking Backwards*. New York: Dover Publications
Blackley, W. (1885) *Thrift and Independence*. London: E. and J.B. Young
Blankenhorn, D. (2008) *Thrift: A Cyclopedia Paperback*. New York: Templeton Foundation Press
Blankenhorn, D., Whitehead, B. and Brophy-Warren, S. (eds) (2009) *Franklin's Thrift: The Lost History of an American Virtue*. West Conshohocken: Templeton Press
Blond, P. (2009) 'Rise of the Red Tories', *Prospect*, 28 February. Available at: www.prospectmagazine.co.uk/magazine/riseoftheredtories. Accessed 27 October 2018.
Bonaiuti, M. (2001) *La Teoria Bioeconomica: La Nuova Economia di N. Georgescu-Roegen*. Rome: Carocci
Bonaiuti, M. (2005) *Obiettivo Decrescita. Editrice Missionaria Italiana*. Bologna: Editrice Missionaria Italiana

Bonaiuti, M. (2014) *The Great Transition*. London: Routledge
Bonhoeffer, D. (1959) *The Cost of Discipleship*. London: Simon & Schuster
Boulding, K. (1964) *The Meaning of the Twentieth Century: The Great Transition*. New York: HarperCollins
Boyer, R. (1990) *Regulation Theory*. London: Routledge
Bradshaw, A. (2019, forthcoming) 'Austerity and the Fetish of the Guilty Consumer', *Journal of Consumer Culture*
Bramall, R. (2013) *The Cultural Politics of Austerity: Past and Present in Austere Times*. London: Palgrave Macmillan
Briggs, A. (2000) *Go To It! Working for Victory on the Home Front 1939–1945*. London: Mitchell Beazley/Imperial War Museum
Briggs, S. (1975) *Keep Smiling Through: The Home Front 1939–1945*. London: George Weidenfeld and Nicolson
Brogan, B. (2010) 'My Advice to David Cameron', *Telegraph*, 29 April. Available at: www.telegraph.co.uk/news/election-2010/7653636/Boris-Johnson-interview-My-advice-to-David-Cameron-Ive-made-savings-so-can-you.html. Accessed 16 March 2017.
Burnett, J. (1986) *A Social History of Housing, 1815–1985*. London: Methuen
Burns, J. (1894) Address to British TUC
Calder, L. (2013) 'Saving and Spending', in Trentmann, Frank (ed.) *The Oxford Handbook of the History of Consumption*. Oxford: Oxford University Press
Calvin, J. (2007) *Institutes*. Peabody: Hendrickson Publishers
Calvin, J. (2015) *To the Christian Nobility*. London: Scriptura Press
Campbell, C. (2005) *The Romantic Ethic and the Spirit of Modern Consumerism*. York: Alcuin Academics
Carpenter, J. (2003) 'New England's Puritan Century: Three Generations of Continuity in the City upon a Hill', *Fides Et Historia*, vol. 35(1), pp. 41–58
Carruthers, D. (2001) 'From Opposition to Orthodoxy: The Remaking of Sustainable Development', *Journal of Third World Studies*, vol. 18(2), pp. 93–122
Carson, R. (1962) *Silent Spring*. New York: Houghton Mifflin Company
Carter, S. (2012) *The Frugal Housewife*. Lexington: ULAN Press
Carwardine, R. (2001) 'Charles Sellers's Antinominas and Arminians: Methodists and the Market Revolution', in Noll, M. (ed.) *God and Mammon: Protestants, Money and the Market*. Oxford: Oxford University Press
Castells, M. (1977) *The Urban Question*. Cambridge, MA: MIT Press
Cattaneo, C., D'Alisa, G., Kallis, G. and Zografos, C. (2012) 'Degrowth Futures and Democracy', *Futures*, vol. 44, pp. 515–523
Cavell, S. (1922) *The Senses of Walden*. Chicago: Chicago University Press
Channing, W. (2010) *Self-Culture, an Address by W. E. Channing*. Whitefish: Kessinger Publishing
Child, L. (2016) [1832] *The American Frugal Housewife*. North Charleston: CreateSpace Independent Publishing Platform
Clarke, J. and Newman, J. (2012) 'The Alchemy of Austerity', *Critical Social Policy*, vol. 32(3), pp. 299–319
Clausen, C. (1993) 'How to Join the Middle Classes with the Help of Dr. Smiles and Mrs. Beeton', *American Scholar*, vol. 62, pp. 403–418
Cohen, L. (2003) *A Consumers' Republic*. New York: Vintage Books
Coleman, S. and Collins, P. (2000) 'The "Plain" and the "Positive": Ritual, Experience and Aesthetics in Quakerism and Charismatic Christianity', *Journal of Contemporary Religion*, vol. 15(3), pp. 317–332

Crapsey, A. S. (1914) *The Rise of the Working Class*. Whitefish: Kessinger Publishing
Crogan, P. (2010) 'Knowledge, Care and Trans-Individuation: An Interview with Bernard Stiegler', *Cultural Politics*, vol. 6(2), pp. 157–170
Curtis, F. (2003) 'Eco-Localism and Sustainability', *Ecological Economics*, vol. 46(1), pp. 83–102
Daniels, B. (1995) *Puritans at Play: Leisure and Recreation in Colonial New England*. London: Macmillan Press
Davies, A. (2000) *The Quakers in English Society*. Oxford: Oxford University Press
Davis, J. and Mathewes, C. (2011) 'Saving Grace and Moral Striving: Thrift in Puritan Theology', in Yates, J. and Hunter, J. (eds) *Thrift and Thriving in America: Capitalism and the Moral Order from the Puritans to the Present*. New York: Oxford University Press
De Geus, M. (2003) *The End of Over-Consumption: Towards a Lifestyle of Moderation and Self-Restraint*. Utrecht: International Books
De Graaf, J. (2003) *Take Back Your Time: Fighting Overwork and Time Poverty in America*. San Francisco: Berrett-Koehler
Demaria, F. and Kothari, A. (2017) 'The Post-Development Dictionary Agenda: Paths to the Pluriverse', *Third World Quarterly*, vol. 38(12), pp. 2588–2599
de Riveros, O. (2001) *The Myth of Development: The Non-Viable Economics of the 21st Century*. London: Zed Books
de Tocqueville, A. (2003) *Democracy in America*. London: Penguin
Dickens, C. (1992) [1850] *David Copperfield*. London: Wordsworth Editions
Dickens, C. (1996) [1857] *Little Dorrit*. London: Wordsworth Editions
Dickens, C. (2013) [1848] *The Life and Adventures of Nicholas Nickleby*. London: Chapman and Hall
Ding, Z. (2008) 'From Self-Reform to Social Reform: A Study of Thoreau's Social and Political Thoughts', *Canadian Social Science*, vol. 4(4), pp. 37–44
Disraeli, B. (2016) [1845] *Sybil, or The Two Nations*. North Charleston: CreateSpace Independent Publishing Platform
Doherty, D. and Etzioni, A. (2003) *Voluntary Simplicity*. Oxford: Rowman & Littlefield
Dominguez, J. and Robin, V. (1992) *Your Money or Your Life*. New York: Penguin
Dorey, P. (1995) *The Conservative Party and the Trade Unions*. London: Psychology Press
Douthwaite, R. (1992) *The Growth Illusion: How Economic Growth has Enriched the Few, Impoverished the Many and Endangered the Planet*. Dublin: Lilliput Press
Durning, A. (1992) *How Much is Enough? The Consumer Society and the Future of the Earth*. New York: W. W. Norton
Eaton, D. (2013) 'The Economists of the Reformation: An Overview of Reformation Teaching Concerning Work, Wealth, and Interest', *Sage Open*, July–September, pp. 1–9
Ege, R. and Igersheim, H. (2011) *Freedom and Happiness in Economic Thought and Philosophy*. London: Routledge
Ehrman, E. (2003) *Dressed Neat and Plain: The Clothing of John Wesley and His Teaching on Dress Paperback*. London: John Wesley's House and the Museum of Methodism
Elgin, D. (1993) *Voluntary Simplicity: Towards a Way of Life that is Outwardly Simple and Inwardly Rich*. New York: William Morrow
Elgin, D., and Mitchell, A. (1977) 'Voluntary Simplicity', *Co-Evolutionary Quarterly*. Available at: www.simpleliving. net/awakeningearth/pdf/voluntary_simplicity.pdf. Accessed 23 May 2018.
Emerson, R. (1841) 'Man the Reformer', *The Dial*. Available at: www.bartleby.com/5/103.html. Accessed 22 April 2018.

Escobar, A. (1995) *Encountering Development*. Princeton: Princeton University Press
Escobar, A. (2015) 'De-Growth, Post-Development, and Transitions: A Preliminary Conversation', *Sustainability Science*, vol. 10(3), pp. 451–462
Etzioni, A. (1998) 'Voluntary Simplicity: Characterization, Select Psychological Implications, and Societal Consequences', *Journal of Economic Psychology*, vol. 19, pp. 619–643
Evans, D. (2011) 'Thrifty, Green or Frugal: Reflections on Sustainable Consumption in a Changing Economic Climate', *Geoforum*, vol. 42, pp. 550–557
Falk, P. and Campbell, C. (1997) *The Shopping Experience*. London: Sage
Fanon, F. (1986) *Black Skin, White Masks*. London: Pluto
Fournier, V. (2008) 'Escaping from the Economy: The Politics of De-Growth', *International Journal of Sociology and Social Policy*, vol. 28(11/12), pp. 528–545
Fox, G. (1803) *Journal of George Fox*. Richmond: Friends United Press
Franklin, B. (1728) *Articles of Belief and Acts of Religion*. Available at: franklinpapers.org/franklin/framedVolumes.jsp?vol=1&page=101a. Accessed 27 November 2018.
Franklin, B. (2012a) *Poor Richard's Almanac*. North Charleston: CreateSpace Independent Publishing Platform
Franklin, B. (2012b) *The Autobiography of Benjamin Franklin*. North Charleston: CreateSpace Independent Publishing Platform
Fraser, S. (2011) 'The Rise and Fall of Collective Thrift', in Yates, J. and Hunter, J. (eds) *Thrift and Thriving in America: Capitalism and the Moral Order from the Puritans to the Present*. New York: Oxford University Press
Frazer, G. (2015) *Methodism: Its History, Teaching, and Government*. South Yarra: Leopold Classic Library
Frazier, E. (2002) *Black Bourgeoisie*. Columbia: University of Missouri Press
Friesen, V. (1984) *The Spirit of the Huckleberry: Sensuousness in Thoreau*. Edmonton: University of Alberta Press
Fritsch, A. (1974) *The Contrasumers: A Citizen's Guide to Resource Conservation*. New York: Praeger
Galbraith, J. (1958) *The Affluent Society*. London: Penguin
Gardiner, J. (2004) *Wartime: Britain 1939–1945*. London: Headline Book Publishing
Garrett, M. (2013) 'The Self-Made Son: Social Competition and the Vanishing Mother' in Franklin's Autobiography', *Early American Literature*, vol. 80(2), pp. 519–542
Georgescu-Roegen, N. (1971) *The Entropy Law and the Economic Process*. Cambridge, MA: Harvard University Press
Georgescu-Roegen, N. (2004) *La Décroissance*. Paris: Sang de la Terre
Gibson-Graham, J.K. (2006) *A Postcapitalist Politics*. Minneapolis: University of Minnesota Press
Ginn, F. (2012) 'Dig for Victory! New Histories of Wartime Gardening in Britain', *Journal of Historical Geography*, vol. 38(3), pp. 294–305
Gorz, A. (1975) *Ecology and Freedom*. Paris: Galilée
Gregg, R. (1936) *The Value of Voluntary Simplicity*. Wallingford: Pendle Hill
Grigsby, M. (2004) *Buying Time and Getting By: The Voluntary Simplicity Movement*. Albany: State University of New York Press
Grusin, R. (1993) 'Thoreau, Extravagance, and the Economy of Nature', *American Literary History*, vol. 5(1), pp. 30–50
Harding, W. (1991) 'Thoreau's Sexuality', *Journal of Homosexuality*, vol. 21(3), pp. 23–45
Harvey, D. (2007) *A Brief History of Neoliberalism*. Oxford: Oxford University Press

Hathaway, M. and Boff, L. (2009) *The Tao of Liberation: Exploring the Ecology of Transformation*. New York: Orbis Books
Hatherley, O. (2016) *Ministry of Nostalgia*. London: Verso
Hayek, F. A. (1982) *Law, Legislation and Liberty. Volume 2: The Mirage of Social Justice*. London: Routledge
Hendrick, G. (1956) 'The Influence of Thoreau's "Civil Disobedience" on Gandhi's Satyagraha', *The New England Quarterley*, vol. 29(4), pp. 462–471
Hennessy, P. (1993) *Never Again: Britain 1945–1951*. London: Vintage Books
Heywood, A. (2007) *Political Ideologies*. London: Palgrave Macmillan
Hinton, E. and Redclift, M. (2009) 'Austerity and Sufficiency: The Changing Politics of Sustainable Consumption'. Politics and Development Working Paper Series, Department of Geography, King's College London Environment, 17, 1–22. Available at: www.kcl.ac.uk/schools/sspp/geography/research/epd/working.html. Accessed 7 June 2017.
Hirsch, F. (1976) *Social Limits to Growth*. London: Routledge
Hirschman, A. (1977) *The Passions and the Interests*. New York: Princeton University Press
Hobson, J., and Mummery, A. (1889) *Physiology of Industry*. London: Routledge
Hoffer, M. (2003) *The Games We Played: The Golden Age of Board and Table Games*. New York: Princeton Architectural Press
Hulme, A. (2016) 'F**k the Cupcake Revolution! David Cameron, Samuel Smiles, and the Geographies of Neo-Victorian Thrift', *Antipode*, vol. 48(4). Available at: https://antipodefoundation.org/2016/06/07/fk-the-cupcake-revolution/. Accessed 5 January 2019.
Huneke, M. (2005) 'The Face of the Un-Consumer: An Empirical Examination of the Practice of Voluntary Simplicity in the United States', *Psychology and Marketing*, vol. 22(7), pp. 527–550
Hylson-Smith, K. (1992) *Evangelicals in the Church of England 1734–1984*. London: Bloomsbury
Illich, I. (1973) *Tools for Conviviality*. London: Calder and Boyars
Illich, I. (1977) *Towards a History of Needs*. New York: Pantheon Books
Isaacson, W. (2003) *Benjamin Franklin: An American Life*. New York: Simon & Schuster
Jackson, T. (2016) *Prosperity Without Growth: Foundations for the Economy of Tomorrow*. London: Routledge
Jakubowski, M. (2011) 'The Open Source Ecology Paradigm'. Available at: http://opensourceecology.org/wiki/Open_Source_Ecology_Paradigm. Accessed 16 February 2018.
Jarvis, A. (1997) *Samuel Smiles and the Construction of Victorian Values*. Stroud: Sutton Publishing
Jessop, B. and Sum, N.-L. (2006) *Beyond the Regulation Approach: Putting Capitalist Economies in Their Place*. Cheltenham: Edward Elgar
Jevons, W. (1865) *The Coal Question: An Inquiry Concerning the Progress of the Nation and the Probable Exhaustion of Our Coal-Mines*. New York: Augustus M. Kelly
Kallis, Giorgos (2015) 'The Left Should Embrace De-Growth', *The New Internationalist*, 11 November. Available at: www.countercurrents.org/kalis111115.htm. Accessed 9 May 2018.
Keynes, J. M. (1964) *The General Theory of Employment, Interest and Money*. London: Macmillan
Kiaer, C. (2005) *Imagine No Possessions: The Socialist Objects of Russian Constructivism*. Cambridge, MA: MIT Press

King, M. (2014) *Quakernomics: An Ethical Capitalism*. London: Anthem Press
Kruze, K. (2016) *One Nation Under God: How Corporate America Invented Christian America*. New York: Basic Books
Kynaston, D. (2008) *Austerity Britain, 1945–51*. New York: Walker and Company
Kynaston, D. (2010) 'Austerity was a Hard Sell in the 40s: Today it's Harder Still', *Guardian*, 21 June. Available at: www.theguardian.com/commentisfree/2010/jun/21/austerity-hard-sell-budget-2010. Accessed 14 July 2017.
Lastovicka, J., Bettencourt, L., Hughner, R. and Kuntze, R. (1999) 'Lifestyle of the Tight and Frugal: Theory and Measurement', *Journal of Consumer Behaviour*, vol. 26, pp. 85–97
Latouche, S. (2003) 'Le marche, l'agora et l'acropole: Se reapproprier le marche', *Refractions*, vol. 9, pp. 17–26
Latouche, S. (2004a) *Survivre au Développement*. Paris: Mille et une Nuit
Latouche, S. (2004b) 'De-Growth Economics: Why Less Should be Much More', *Le Monde Diplomatique*, November. Available at: https://mondediplo.com/2004/11/14latouche. Accessed 9 May 2018.
Latouche, S. (2005) *Décoloniser L'immaginaire*. Lyon: Parangon
Latouche, S. (2010a) 'De-Growth', *Journal of Cleaner Production*, vol. 18, pp. 519–522
Latouche, S. (2010b) *Farewell to Growth*. London: Polity
Latouche, S. (2010c) *Sortir de la Société de Consommation*. Paris: Les Liens qui Libèrent
Lawrence, D. (1933) 'Benjamin Franklin', in *Studies in Classic American Literature*. London: Secker
Lears, J. (1995) *Fables of Abundance: A Cultural History of Advertising in America*. New York: Basic Books
Loftus, D. (2019, forthcoming) 'Thrift, Poverty and Entrepreneurship: The Case of Late-Nineteenth Century London', *New Formations*
Longmate, N. (1971) *How We Lived Then: A History of Everyday Life During the Second World War*. New York: Hutchinson
Luther, M. (2013) *Trade and Usury*. New York: The Classics
Lyerly, C. (1998) *Methodism and the Southern Mind, 1770–1810*. Oxford: Oxford University Press
Lynd, R. and Lynd, H. (1937) *Middletown in Transition: A Study in Cultural Conflicts*. New York: Harcourt Brace and Company
Mackay, T. (ed.) (1905) *The Autobiography of Samuel Smiles*. London: John Murray
Malm, A. (2016) *Fossil Capital: The Rise of Steam Power and the Roots of Global Warming*. London: Verso
Mandeville, B. (1997) *The Fable of the Bees*. London: Hackett
Marden, O. (1899) *Thrift, Economy, and Cheerfulness as a Life Power*. Available at: http://manybooks.net/titles/mardenor1839418394-8.html#. Accessed 13 December 2018.
Marx, K. (1859) *A Contribution to the Critique of Political Economy*. Moscow: Progress Publisher
Marx, K. (1961) *Economic and Philosophical Manuscripts*. Moscow: Foreign Language Publications House
Marx, L. (1964) *The Machine in the Garden: Technology and the Pastoral Ideal in America*. London: Oxford University Press
Masferrer-Dodas, E., Rico-Garcia, L., Huanca, T. and Reyes-García, V. (2011) 'Consumption of Market Goods and Wellbeing in Small-Scale Societies: An Empirical Test among the Tsimane' in the Bolivian Amazon', *Ecological Economics*, vol. 84, pp. 213–220
Mather, C. (1692) *Ornaments for the Daughters of Zion, or the Character and Happiness of a Vertuous Woman*. Boston: Samuel Phillips

Mayer, R. (1989) *The Consumer Movement: Guardians of the Marketplace*. University of Michigan: Twayne Publishers

McCarthy, K. (2011) 'Spreading the Gospel of Self-Denial: Thrift and Association in Antebellum America', in Yates, J. and Hunter, J. (eds) *Thrift and Thriving in America: Capitalism and the Moral Order from the Puritans to the Present*. New York: Oxford University Press

McIntosh, J. (1974) *Thoreau as Romantic Naturalist: His Shifting Stance toward Nature*. New York: Cornell University Press

McKay, E. (2008) '"For Refreshment and Preservinge Health": The Definition and Function of Recreation in Early Modern England', *Historical Research*, vol. 81(211), pp. 52–74

McKendrick, N., Brewer, J. and Plumb, J. (1984) *The Birth of a Consumer Society*. London: HarperCollins

McRobbie, A. (2008) 'Young Women and Consumer Culture', *Cultural Studies*, vol. 22(5), pp. 531–550

McWilliam, D. (2016) 'London's Dispossessed: Questioning the Neo-Victorian Politics of Neoliberal Austerity in Richard Warlow's *Ripper Street*', *Victoriographies*, vol. 6(1), pp. 42–61

Meadows, D., Meadows, D. and Randes, J. (1972) *Limits to Growth*. New York: Universe Books

Mencken, H. (2015) *A Book of Prefaces*. South Yarra: Leopold Classic Library

Merton, R. (1947) *Mass Persuasion: The Social Psychology of a War Bond Drive*. New York: Harper and Brothers

Michaelis, L. (2008) 'Quaker Simplicity', in Bouckart, L., Opdebeeck, H. and Zsolnay, L. (eds) *Frugality: Rebalancing Material and Spiritual Values in Economic Life*. Oxford: Verglag Peter Lang

Mill, J. (1844) *On the Definition of Political Economy, and on the Method of Investigation Proper to it*. London: John W. Parker

Miller, D. (2013) *A Theory of Shopping*. London: John Wiley and Sons

Miller, P. (1939) *The New England Mind: The Seventeenth Century*. New York: Macmillan

Milne, M., Kearing, K. and Walton, S. (2006) 'Creating Adventures in Wonderland: The Journey Metaphor and Environmental Sustainability', *Organization*, vol. 13(6), pp. 801–839

Montesquieu, Charles-Louis de Secondat (2002) *The Spirit of the Laws*. Cambridge: Cambridge University Press

Morris, R. (1981) 'Samuel Smiles and the Genesis of Self Help: The Retreat to a Petit Bourgeois Utopia', *The Historical Journal*, vol. 24(1), pp. 89–109

Morris, W. (1884) 'Art and Socialism' lecture, 23 January. Available at: www.marxists.org/archive/morris/works/1884/as/as.htm. Accessed 6 May 2018.

Mort, F. (2006) 'Competing Domains: Democratic Subjects and Consuming Subjects', in Trentmann, Frank (ed.) *The Making of the Consumer*. Oxford: Berg

Murray, C. (2015) *Losing Ground*. New York: Basic Books

Nachane, D. (n.d.) 'Gandhian Economic Thought and its Influence on Economic Policymaking in India'. Available at: www.researchgate.net/publication/228587596_Gandhian_Economic_Thought_and_Its_Influence_on_Economic_Policymaking_in_India. Accessed 2 December 2018.

Nash, J. (1995) 'Toward the Revival and Reform of the Subversive Virtue: Frugality', *Annual of the Society of Christian Ethics*, pp. 137–160

Newman, L. (2003) 'Thoreau's Natural Community and Utopian Socialism', *American Literature*, vol. 75(3), pp. 515–544

Newman, L. (2004) 'Thoreau's Materialism: From Walden to Wild Fruits', *Nineteenth-Century Prose*, vol. 31(2), pp. 105–137

Noll, M. (2001) *God and Mammon*. Oxford: Oxford University Press

Odum, H. and Odum, E. (2001) *A Prosperous Way Down*. Boulder: University of Colorado Press

OECD (2002) *Towards Sustainable Household Consumption? Trends and Policies in OECD Countries*. Paris: OECD

Oelschlaeger, M. (1991) *The Idea of Wilderness*. New Haven: Yale University Press

Ossowaska, M. (1986) *Bourgeois Morality*. London: Routledge and Kegan Paul

Packard, V. (1970) *The Waste Makers*. London: Penguin

Parkin, K. (2006) *Food is Love: Advertising and Gender Roles in Modern America*. Philadelphia: University of Philadelphia Press

Parrington, V. (1927) *Main Currents in American Thought*. New York: Harcourt, Brace and Company

Patten, S. (1968) *The New Basis of Civilization*. Cambridge, MA: Harvard University Press

Paulson, S. (2017) 'De-Growth: Culture, Power and Change', *Journal of Political Ecology*, vol. 24, pp. 425–448

Penn, W. (2016) *No Cross, No Crown: A Discourse, Shewing the Nature and Discipline of the Holy Cross of Christ*. London: Forgotten Books

Philibert, J. (1990) 'The Politics of Tradition: Toward a Generic Culture in Vanuatu', in Manning, F. and Philibert, J. (eds) *Customs in Conflict*. Peterborough, Ontario: Broadview

Pierce, L. (2003) 'What is Voluntary Simplicity?' Available at: www.gallagherpress.com/pierce/whatisvs.htm. Accessed 18 May 2018.

Polanyi, K. (1944). *The Great Transformation*. New York: Farrar and Reinhart

Polimeni, J., Mayumi, K., Giampietro, M. and Alcott, B. (2008) *The Myth of Resource Efficiency: The Jevons Paradox*. London: Earthscan

Potter, D. (1954) *People of Plenty: Economic Abundance and the American Character*. Chicago: Chicago University Press

Rael, P. (2011) 'African Americans, Slavery, and Thrift', in Yates, J. and Hunter, J. (eds) *Thrift and Thriving in America: Capitalism and the Moral Order from the Puritans to the Present*. New York: Oxford University Press

Rahnema, M. and Bawtree, V. (1997) *The Post-Development Reader*. London: Zed

Randall, R. (2009) 'Loss and Climate Change: The Cost of Parallel Narrative', *Ecopsychology*, vol. 1(3), pp. 118–129

Raskin, P., Banuri, T., Gallopin, G., Gutman, P., Hammond, A., Kates, R. and Swart, R. (2002) *Great Transition*. Boston: Stockholm Environment Institute. Available at: www.gtinitiative.org/documents/Great_Transitions.pdf. Accessed 15 January 2018.

Ripley, G. (2007) 'Letter to Ralph Waldo Emerson, 9th November, 1840', in Frothingham, O., *George Ripley*. Whitefish: Kessinger Publishing

Rist, G. (2014) *History of Development*. London: Zed

Roberts, S. (2015) *Puritanism and the Pursuit of Happiness*. Woodbridge: Boydell and Brewer

Rodchenko, A., Stepanova, V. and Noever, P. (eds) (1991) *Aleksandr Rodchenko and Varvara Stepanova: The Future is Our Only Goal*. Munich: Prestel

Roiland, D. (2016) 'Frugality, A Positive Principle to Promote Sustainable Development', *Journal of Agricultural and Environmental Ethics*, vol. 29, pp. 571–585

Roosevelt, F. (1938) 'Acceptance of the Re-nomination for the Presidency Speech, Philadelphia, June 27th', in *The Public Papers and Addresses of Franklin D Roosevelt*. New York: Random House
Sachs, W. (2009) *The Development Dictionary*. London: Zed
Schlink, F. and Chase, S. (1927) *Your Money's Worth*. New York: Macmillan and Company
Schlink, F. and Kallet, A. (1933) *One Hundred Million Guinea Pigs*. New York: Vanguard Press
Schneider, F., Martinez-Alier, J. and Kallis, G. (2011) 'Sustainable Growth', *Journal of Industrial Ecology*, vol. 15(5), pp. 654–656
Schor, J. (1998) *The Overspent American: Upscaling, Downshifting, and the New Consumer*. New York: Basic Books
Schumacher, E. (1973) *Small is Beautiful: Economics as if People Mattered*. London: Blong and Briggs
Scott-Cato, M. (2006) *Market, Schmarket: Building the Post-Capitalist Economy*. Cheltenham: New Clarion Press
Seabrook, J. (1993) *Victims of Development*. London: Verso
Shaw, D. and Newholm, T. (2002) 'Voluntary Simplicity and the Ethics of Consumption', *Psychology and Marketing*, vol. 19, pp. 167–185
Sherry, F. (1990) 'A Sociocultural Analysis of a Mid-Western American Flea Market', *Journal of Consumer Research*, vol. 17(1), pp. 13–30
Shi, D. (2007) *The Simple Life: Plain Living and High Thinking in American Culture*. Athens: University of Georgia Press
Shukaitis, S. (2013) 'Can the Object Become a Comrade', *Ephemera*, vol. 13(2), pp. 437–444
Simondon, G. (2017) *On the Mode of Existence of Technical Objects*. Minneapolis: University of Minnesota Press
Singh, B. (2010) 'Asceticism and Eroticism in Gandhi, Thoreau and Nietzsche: An Essay in Geo-Philosophy', *Borderlands*, vol. 9(3). Available at: www.borderlands.net.au/vol9no3_2010/singh_asceticism.pdf. Accessed 15 December 2018.
Singley, C. (2019, forthcoming) 'Thrift and Thriftlessness in Edith Wharton's *The House of Mirth*', *New Formations*
Sissons, M. and French, P. (1964) *The Age of Austerity*. London: Penguin Books
Skeggs, B. and Wood, H. (2012) *Reacting to Reality Television: Performance, Audience and Value*. Abingdon: Routledge
Sklair, L. (2016) 'Half-Baked', *Philosophica Critica*, vol. 2(2), pp. 103–116
Sleeper, J. (2015) 'Our Puritan Heritage', *Democracy*, vol. 37, pp. 56–70
Smiles, S. (1839) 'The Education of the People (A Review of Channing's Self-Help)', *Leeds Times*, 23 February
Smiles, S. (1857) *The Life of George Stephenson, Railway Engineer*. London: John Murray
Smiles, S. (2007) *Thrift*. Whitefish: Kessinger Publishing
Smiles, S. (2012) *Self-Help*. London: Forgotten Books
Smith, A. (2003) [1776] *The Wealth of Nations*. London: Bantam Classics
Smith, J. (2014) *A Concise History of the New Deal*. Cambridge: Cambridge University Press
Soddy, F. (1922) *Cartesian Economics: The Bearing of Physical Science Upon State Stewardship*. London: Henderson
Soddy, F. (1926) *Wealth, Virtual Wealth and Debt*. London: George Allen and Unwin
Spratt, S., Simms, A., Neitzert, E. and Ryan-Collins, R. (2009) *The Great Transition*. London: New Economics Foundation

Stachniewski, J. (1991) *The Persecutory Imagination*. London: Clarendon Press
Stiegler, B. (2004) *Mécréance et Discrédit: Tome 1, La décadence des démocraties industrielles*. Paris: Editions Galilée
Stiegler, B. (2006a) *Mécréance et Discrédit: Tome 2, Les sociétés incontrolables d'individus désaffectés*. Paris: Editions Galilée
Stiegler, B. (2006b) *Mécréance et Discrédit: Tome 3, L'esprit perdu du capitalisme*. Paris: Editions Galilée
Stoller, L. (1957) *After Walden: Thoreau's Changing Views on Economic Man*. New York: Stanford University Press
Tawney, R. (2015) *Religion and the Rise of Capitalism*. London: Verso
Templeton, J. (2011) *Thrift and Generosity: The Joy of Giving*. Whittier: Templeton Press.
Tholfsen, T. (1971) 'The Intellectual Origins of Mid-Victorian Stability', *Political Science Quarterly*, vol. 76, pp. 58–88
Thompson, E. (1963) *The Making of the English Working Class*. London: Pelican
Thoreau, H. (1985) *A Week on the Concord and Merrimack Rivers / Walden / The Maine Woods / Cape Cod*. New York: Library of America
Thoreau, H. (2001) *Wild Fruits*. New York: W.W. Norton and Company
Thoreau, H. (2004) *Civil Disobedience*. New York: The Ivy Press
Thoreau, H. (2012) *Walden*. London: Penguin
Titmuss, R. (1962) *Income Distribution and Social Change*. London: Allen & Unwin
Trainer, T. (2000) 'Where Are We, Where Do We Want to Be, and How Do We Get There?', *Democracy and Nature*, vol.6(2), pp. 267–286
Travers, T. (1977) 'Samuel Smiles and the Origins of Self-Help: Reform and the New Enlightenment', *Albion*, vol. 9(2), pp. 161–187
Trendafilov, V. (2015) 'The Origins of Self-Help: Samuel Smiles and the Formative Influences on an Ex-Seminal Work', *The Victorian*. Available at: http://journals.sfu.ca/vict/index.php/vict/article/viewFile/148/73. Accessed 3 January 2018.
Tucker, D. (1990) *The Decline of Thrift in America*. New York: Praeger
Twain, M. (1870) 'The Late Benjamin Franklin', *The Galaxy*, pp. 138–140
Tyrrell, A. (1970) 'The Origins of a Victorian Bestseller: An Unacknowledged Debt', *Notes and Queries*, vol. 17(9), pp. 347–349
UNDP (1998) *Human Development Report*. Oxford: Oxford University Press
Vanderbilt, T. (1996) 'It's a Wonderful (Simplified) Life: Is the Voluntary Simplicity Movement True Liberation, or Diminished Expectations Under Another Name?', *The Nation*, vol. 262(3), 22 January.
Veblen, T. (1994) *Theory of the Leisure Class*. New York: Dover Publications
Verbrugge, V. and Krell, K. (2015) *Paul and Money: A Biblical and Theological Analysis of the Apostle's Teachings and Practices*. Michigan: Zondervan
Waller, J. and Vaughan-Rees, M. (1987) *Women in Wartime: The Role of Women's Magazines 1939–1945*. London: Macdonald
Walls, L. (1995) *Seeing New Worlds*. Madison: University of Wisconsin Press
Walther, C., Sandlin, J. and Wuensch, K. (2016) 'Voluntary Simplifiers, Spirituality, and Happiness', *Humanity and Society*, vol. 40(1), pp. 22–42
Watkins, T. (2010) *The Great Depression: America in the 1930s*. Boston: Back Bay
Weber, M. (1992) *The Protestant Ethic and the Spirit of Capitalism*. London: Routledge
Wesley, J. (1786) *Thoughts upon Methodism*. Available at: www.imarc.cc/one_meth/vol-02-no-02.html. Accessed 6 May 2018.
Wesley, J. (1961) *On the Uses of Money*. London: Epworth Press

Wilde, O. (2001) *The Soul of a Man Under Socialism*. London: Penguin
Wilk, R. (2001) 'Consuming Morality', *Journal of Consumer Culture*, vol. 2(1), pp. 245–260
Winship, J. (1987) *Inside Woman's Magazines*. London: Pandora
Witherington, B. (2012) *Jesus and Money*. Ada: Brazos Press.
Witkowski, T. (2010) 'A Brief History of Frugality Discourses in the United States', *Consumption Markets and Culture*, vol. 13(3), pp. 235–258
Yates, J. and Hunter, J. (eds) (2011) *Thrift and Thriving in America: Capitalism and the Moral Order from the Puritans to the Present*. New York: Oxford University Press
Zavestoski, S. (2002) 'The Social-Psychological Bases of Anti-Consumption Attitudes', *Psychology and Marketing*, vol. 19, pp. 121–126

Index

abundance 13–14, 15, 16
advertising 13, 32, 72, 80–81
African-American 74, 83–84
American Dream 38–39
anarchism 24, 61
Anthropocene 93–94, 100–101, 117–118
anti-capitalist 60, 83, 94, 115–116, 118
Aquinas, Thomas 22–23
Aristotle 9, 18, 23, 38, 110
asceticism 17–18, 23, 41, 54, 56–57, 58, 61
Augustine, Saint 22, 45
austerity 26, 41, 48, 51–52, 68–69, 76–78, 89, 107, 115, 123
avarice 22, 39, 47, 86, 110

bargain 1, 10, 73
Bellamy, Edward 80
Bellamy clubs 80
Berle, Adolf 81
Bhagavad Gita 56
Big Society 47, 112
Blitz spirit 77
buen vivir 98
Brains Trust 81–82, 85
Brook Farm 63–65, 68, 110, 111, 117
Brundtland report 92

Calvin, Jean 18–22, 24, 27–28, 37, 44–45
Cameron, David 47–48, 51–52, 76–77, 112
capitalocentrism 12
Catholic 17, 20, 52, 78
Channing, William 45, 66
charity 18, 24, 28, 30, 32, 47, 58
Chartists 43–44
Chase, Stuart 80
Club of Rome 92
collective commodities 111, 112, 113
collectivism 33, 62, 64–66
Confucius 104

Conservative Party 50–51
conspicuous consumption 13, 80, 83–84, 103
constructivists 112
consumer capitalism 10–11, 15, 32–33, 95, 104
consumerism 7–8, 12, 13, 15, 42, 49, 77–78, 87–88, 91
consumer revolution 12, 13
conviviality 98, 102
credit 20, 50, 89

Darwin, Charles 62, 110
debt 21, 25, 37, 39, 41–42, 77–78, 89–90
decencies 13, 40
Defoe, Daniel 40
de-growth 94–110, 113, 118
democracy 32, 36, 65, 73–74, 98, 102
Democrat 81
de Tocqueville, Alexis 32, 88
developing world 16, 92, 118
Dewey, John 80
Dickens, Charles 40–41
Disraeli, Benjamin 50–52
Douglas, Paul 80

Ecological Swaraj 98
ecological thrift 11
economic man 7, 9, 22
economic recovery 81
Efficiency Movement 80
Emergency Powers Act 69
Emerson, Ralph Waldo 45–47, 53–54, 63, 68
Enlightenment 44, 50, 66–99
ethical consumption 26, 32
eudaimonia 38, 110

Fable of the Bees 85
fireside chats 75, 83
First World War 32, 75

food banks 107
fossil fuel 92, 94
Fourier, Charles 64
Fox, George 24–25
Frankfurt School 14–15, 117
Franklin, Benjamin 33, 35–48, 52, 56, 58
freedom 38, 47–48, 52, 54, 58, 63, 73, 87–88, 98–99, 116
functionalism 51

Game of Life 42
Gandhi, Mahatma 56–57, 61, 99, 104
Global Village Construction Set 96–97
Glorious Revolution 21
Great Depression 32, 79–82
Gross National Happiness 98

Hayek, Friedrich 24, 86–87
home front 76
Hoover, Herbert 80–81

idealism 62, 65, 111, 115
individualism 24, 31, 33, 34, 40, 44–47, 51, 61–67, 69, 77, 80, 113, 115, 116
industrialisation 13, 50
interventionism 85

Jevons Paradox 102

Keynes, John Maynard 85–88
Keynesianism 85, 89, 100

Labour Party 49
laissez-faire 24
Lawrence, D. H. 38
Lloyd George, David 83
localism 25
Luddite 111
Luther, Martin 18–20
luxuries 13, 58, 68

marketing 87, 107, 114
Marxism 110
materialism 62, 65, 66
Mather, Cotton 17, 21, 36
May, Theresa 50, 51
mechanisation 13
Methodists 17, 27–31, 34

middle class 13, 35, 39, 40, 42, 44, 45, 48, 68, 80, 83, 106, 117
Ministry of Information 69
modernity 14, 16, 88, 89, 101
Moley, Raymond 81
moralism 35, 49, 77
morals 8, 11, 14, 15, 36, 48

National Industrial Recovery Act 82
National Recovery Administration 82
National Thrift Movement 50
nature 23, 53–54, 57, 59, 61–62, 67–68, 96, 99
neo-Victorian 50, 52, 75
New Deal 33, 81–85, 90–91
New Right 52
niceties 40
nostalgia 75–76, 78, 111

O'Connor, Basil 81
One Nationism 50–51
Osborne, George 48, 52, 76, 77

Parable of the Talents 28–29, 31
paradox of thrift 85
Paul, Saint 33–34
Penn, William 24–26
pleasure 6, 7, 10, 17, 18, 88, 114
Poor Richard 36–39
Popular Front 82
post-capitalist 96
poverty 34, 38–39, 45, 48–49, 51, 81, 100, 102, 107, 115
pragmatism 38, 51
predestination 17–19, 24, 27
progress 8, 48, 60
Protestant 8, 12, 19, 33, 35, 56, 59, 74
providentialism 35
Puritans 34, 35, 69, 105

Quakernomics 25
Quakers 17, 24–28, 34, 97

rationing 69, 72–76
recession 76, 78, 95
reciprocal man 22, 99, 116
reciprocity 23, 32, 98, 102, 109, 112–113, 118
Regulation Theory 90

Republican 32, 35, 80, 81, 84
revolution 56, 60, 63, 84, 87, 112
Ripley, George 63–65
Roman Catholic 17
romanticism 12, 56
Roosevelt, Franklin 33, 74–75, 81–83, 85, 88
Ruskin, John 56

saving 6, 7, 8, 9, 10, 17, 29, 31, 47–48, 49, 73, 74, 86, 89
savings bonds 74–75
Say's Law 85, 91
scarcity 13, 74
Schlink, Frederick 80–81
Second World War 69, 72–76, 78, 87–88
self-actualisation 87, 107
self-culture 45, 66–67
self-improvement 38, 43
sensuality 57
shopping 6–7, 9–10, 89
simplicity 60, 64, 76, 77, 78, 103, 107, 118
slavery 31, 54, 58, 65
Smiles, Samuel 39, 41–49, 51, 52, 56, 66, 73, 86
social justice 25, 50, 65, 67, 105
spending 6–10, 13–15, 28, 31, 49, 52, 89, 105, 114
spiritualism 58, 62
stewardship 28, 30, 34, 105
subsistence 27, 67, 97
sustainable development 92, 93, 95, 100

Testimony of Simplicity 25, 26
Thatcher, Margaret 52, 77

thriving 53, 56, 67–68, 89, 97–99, 102, 109–117
time-poverty 90
transcendentalism 46, 53, 56, 62, 68
trickle-down 86, 108
Tugwell, Rexford 81
Twain, Mark 38

Ubuntu 98
underclass 52
underdevelopment 100
unemployment 51, 85, 89
United Nations 92, 100
upper class 59, 80
Uses of Money, The 29, 31
Utopianism 44, 111

Veblen, Thorstein 12, 13, 14, 15, 59, 80
Victorian 35, 40, 42, 44, 45, 49, 50, 69
virtue 8, 13, 32, 36, 42, 84, 86, 93, 109
Voluntary Simplicity 98, 102–110
volunteerism 73, 80

Walden 54–59, 61–62, 64–65, 67
war bonds 74–75
wealth 29, 31, 32, 33, 34, 37, 39, 48, 52, 59, 63, 86, 107–110
Weber, Max 11–12, 19, 21, 33, 39
welfare 1, 52, 78
Wesley, Charles 27
Wesley, John 27–31, 33–34, 105, 137
Wharton, Edith 40–41
working class 27, 30, 45, 47, 48, 49, 51, 52, 59–60, 107, 109

Printed in Australia
AUHW021007020321
342023AU00015B/83